ON CATECHESIS
IN OUR TIME

APOSTOLIC EXHORTATION
CATECHESI TRADENDAE
OF HIS HOLINESS

JOHN PAUL II

TO THE EPISCOPATE, THE CLERGY
AND THE FAITHFUL
OF THE ENTIRE CATHOLIC CHURCH
ON CATECHESIS IN OUR TIME

United States Catholic Conference
Washington, D.C.

Pub. No. 654-9
United States Catholic Conference
Washington, D.C.
ISBN 1-55586-654-9

Text and format from
LIBRERIA EDITRICE VATICANA
Vatican City

Published in the United States, October 1979
Fifth Printing, March 1997

INTRODUCTION

Christ's final command

1. T̶HE CHURCH has always considered
catechesis one of her primary tasks,
for, before Christ ascended to his Father after
his Resurrection, he gave the Apostles a final
command—to make disciples of all nations and
to teach them to observe all that he had com-
manded.[1] He thus entrusted them with the mission and power to proclaim to humanity what
they had heard, what they had seen with their
eyes, what they had looked upon and touched
with their hands, concerning the Word of Life.[2]
He also entrusted them with the mission and
power to explain with authority what he had
taught them, his words and actions, his signs and
commandments. And he gave them the Spirit to
fulfil this mission.

Very soon the name of catechesis was given
to the whole of the efforts within the Church to
make disciples, to help people to believe that
Jesus is the Son of God, so that believing they

[1] Cf. *Mt* 28 : 19-20.
[2] Cf. *1 Jn* 1 : 1.

3

might have life in his name,[3] and to educate and instruct them in this life and thus build up the Body of Christ. The Church has not ceased to devote her energy to this task.

2. The most recent Popes gave catechesis a place of eminence in their pastoral solicitude. Through his gestures, his preaching, his authoritative interpretation of the Second Vatican Council (considered by him the great catechism of modern times), and through the whole of his life, my venerated predecessor Paul VI served the Church's catechesis in a particularly exemplary fashion. On 18 March 1971 he approved the General Catechetical Directory prepared by the Sacred Congregation for the Clergy, a directory that is still the basic document for encouraging and guiding catechetical renewal throughout the Church. He set up the International Council for Catechesis in 1975. He defined in masterly fashion the role and significance of catechesis in the life and mission of the Church when he addressed the participants in the First International Catechetical Congress on 25 September 1971,[4] and he returned explicitly to the subject in his Apostolic Exhortation *Evangelii Nuntiandi*.[5] He decided that catechesis, especially

[3] Cf. *Jn* 20 : 31.
[4] Cf. *AAS.* 63 (1971), pp. 758-764.
[5] Cf. 44; cf. also 45-48 and 54: *AAS* 68 (1976), pp. 34-35; 35-38; 43.

4

that meant for children and young people, should be the theme of the Fourth General Assembly of the Synod of Bishops,[6] which was held in October 1977 and which I myself had the joy of taking part in.

A fruitful Synod

3. At the end of that Synod the Fathers presented the Pope with a very rich documentation, consisting of the various interventions during the Assembly, the conclusions of the working groups, the Message that they had with his consent sent to the people of God,[7] and especially the imposing list of "Propositions" in which they expressed their views on a very large number of aspects of present-day catechesis.

The Synod worked in an exceptional atmosphere of thanksgiving and hope. It saw in catechetical renewal a precious gift from the Holy Spirit to the Church of today, a gift to which the Christian communities at all levels throughout the world are responding with a generosity and inventive dedication that win admiration. The requisite discernment could then be brought to

[6] According to the Motu Proprio *Apostolica Sollicitudo* of 15 September 1965, the Synod of Bishops can come together in General Assembly, in Extraordinary Assembly or in Special Assembly. In the present Apostolic Exhortation the words "Synod", "Synod Fathers" and "Synod Hall" always refer, unless otherwise indicated, to the Fourth General Assembly of the Synod of Bishops on catechesis, held in Rome in October 1977.

[7] Cf. *Synodus Episcoporum, De catechesi hoc nostro tempore tradenda praesertim pueris atque iuvenibus, Ad Populum Dei Nuntius*, e Civitate Vaticana, 28-X-1977; cf. "L'Osservatore Romano", 30 October 1977, pp. 3-4.

bear on a reality that is very much alive and it could benefit from great openness among the people of God to the grace of the Lord and the directives of the Magisterium.

4.   It is in the same climate of faith and hope that I am today addressing this Apostolic Exhortation to you, Venerable Brothers and dear sons and daughters. The theme is extremely vast and the Exhortation will keep to a few only of the most topical and decisive aspects of it, as an affirmation of the happy results of the Synod. In essence, the Exhortation takes up again the reflections that were prepared by Pope Paul VI, making abundant use of the documents left by the Synod. Pope John Paul I, whose zeal and gifts as a catechist amazed us all, had taken them in hand and was preparing to publish them when he was suddenly called to God. To all of us he gave an example of catechesis at once popular and concentrated on the essential, one made up of simple words and actions that were able to touch the heart. I am therefore taking up the inheritance of these two Popes in response to the request which was expressly formulated by the Bishops at the end of the Fourth General Assembly of the Synod and which was welcomed by Pope Paul VI in his closing speech.[8] I am also

8 Cf. *AAS* 69 (1977), p. 633.

doing so in order to fulfil one of the chief duties of my apostolic charge. Catechesis has always been a central care in my ministry as a priest and as a bishop.

I ardently desire that this Apostolic Exhortation to the whole Church should strengthen the solidity of the faith and of Christian living, should give fresh vigour to the initiatives in hand, should stimulate creativity—with the required vigilance—and should help to spread among the communities the joy of bringing the mystery of Christ to the world.

I

WE HAVE BUT ONE TEACHER, JESUS CHRIST

Putting into communion with the Person of Christ

5.   The Fourth General Assembly of the Synod of Bishops often stressed the Christocentricity of all authentic catechesis. We can here use the word "Christocentricity" in both its meanings, which are not opposed to each other or mutually exclusive, but each of which rather demands and completes the other.

In the first place, it is intended to stress that at the heart of catechesis we find, in essence, a Person, the Person of Jesus of Nazareth, "the only Son from the Father ... full of grace and truth",[9] who suffered and died for us and who now, after rising, is living with us forever. It is Jesus who is "the way, and the truth, and the life",[10] and Christian living consists in following Christ, the *sequela Christi*.

The primary and essential object of cateche-

---

[9] *Jn* 1 :14.
[10] *Jn* 14 :6.

8

sis is, to use an expression dear to Saint Paul and also to contemporary theology, "the mystery of Christ". Catechizing is in a way to lead a person to study this Mystery in all its dimensions: "To make all men see what is the plan of the mystery ... comprehend with all the saints what is the breadth and length and height and depth ... know the love of Christ which surpasses knowledge ... (and be filled) with all the fullness of God".[11] It is therefore to reveal in the Person of Christ the whole of God's eternal design reaching fulfilment in that Person. It is to seek to understand the meaning of Christ's actions and words and of the signs worked by him, for they simultaneously hide and reveal his mystery. Accordingly, the definitive aim of catechesis is to put people not only in touch but in communion, in intimacy, with Jesus Christ: only he can lead us to the love of the Father in the Spirit and make us share in the life of the Holy Trinity.

Transmitting Christ's teaching

6. Christocentricity in catechesis also means the intention to transmit not one's own teaching or that of some other master, but the teaching of Jesus Christ, the Truth that he communicates or, to put it more precisely, the Truth that he is.[12] We must therefore say that in catechesis it is Christ, the Incarnate Word and Son of God,

[11] *Eph* 3 :9, 18-19.
[12] Cf. *Jn* 14 :6.

who is taught—everything else is taught with reference to him—and it is Christ alone who teaches—anyone else teaches to the extent that he is Christ's spokesman, enabling Christ to teach with his lips. Whatever be the level of his responsibility in the Church, every catechist must constantly endeavour to transmit by his teaching and behaviour the teaching and life of Jesus. He will not seek to keep directed towards himself and his personal opinions and attitudes the attention and the consent of the mind and heart of the person he is catechizing. Above all, he will not try to inculcate his personal opinions and options as if they expressed Christ's teaching and the lessons of his life. Every catechist should be able to apply to himself the mysterious words of Jesus: "My teaching is not mine, but his who sent me".[13] Saint Paul did this when he was dealing with a question of prime importance: "I received from the Lord what I also delivered to you".[14] What assiduous study of the word of God transmitted by the Church's Magisterium, what profound familiarity with Christ and with the Father, what a spirit of prayer, what detachment from self must a catechist have in order that he can say: "My teaching is not mine"!

[13] *Jn* 7 :16. This is a theme dear to the Fourth Gospel: cf. *Jn* 3:34; 8:28; 12:49-50; 14:24; 17:8, 14.
[14] *1 Cor* 11 :23: the word "deliver" employed here by St Paul was frequently repeated in the Apostolic Exhortation *Evangelii Nuntiandi* to describe the evangelizing activity of the Church, for example 4, 15, 78, 79.

7.   This teaching is not a body of abstract truths.   It is the communication of the living mystery of God.   The person teaching it in the Gospel is altogether superior in excellence to the "masters" in Israel, and the nature of his doctrine surpasses theirs in every way because of the unique link between what he says, what he does and what he is.   Nevertheless, the Gospels clearly relate occasions when Jesus "taught".   "Jesus began to do and teach" [15]—with these two verbs, placed at the beginning of the book of the Acts, Saint Luke links and at the same time distinguishes two poles in Christ's mission.

Jesus taught.   It is the witness that he gives of himself: "Day after day I sat in the Temple teaching".[16]   It is the admiring observation of the evangelists, surprised to see him teaching everywhere and at all times, teaching in a manner and with an authority previously unknown: "Crowds gathered to him again; and again, as his custom was, he taught them";[17] "and they were astonished at his teaching, for he taught them as one who had authority".[18] It is also what his enemies note for the purpose of drawing from it grounds for accusation and

[15] *Acts* 1:1.
[16] *Mt* 26:55; cf. *Jn* 18:20.
[17] *Mk* 10:1.
[18] *Mk* 1:22; cf. also *Mt* 5:2; 11:1; 13:54; 22:16; *Mk* 2:13; 4:1; 6:2, 6; *Lk* 5:3, 17; *Jn* 7:14; 8:2, etc.

11

condemnation: "He stirs up the people, teaching throughout all Judaea, from Galilee even to this place".[19]

The one "Teacher"

8.   One who teaches in this way has a unique title to the name of "Teacher". Throughout the New Testament, especially in the Gospels, how many times is he given this title of Teacher! [20] Of course the Twelve, the other disciples, and the crowds of listeners call him "Teacher" in tones of admiration, trust and tenderness.[21] Even the Pharisees and the Sadducees, the Doctors of the Law, and the Jews in general do not refuse him the title: "Teacher, we wish to see a sign from you";[22] "Teacher, what shall I do to inherit eternal life"? [23] But above all, Jesus himself at particularly solemn and highly significant moments calls himself Teacher: "You call me Teacher and Lord; and you are right, for so I am";[24] and he proclaims the singularity, the uniqueness of his character as Teacher: "You have one teacher",[25] the Christ. One can understand why

[19] Lk 23 : 5.
[20] In nearly fifty places in the four Gospels, this title, inherited from the whole Jewish tradition but here given a new meaning that Christ himself often seeks to emphasize, is attributed to Jesus.
[21] Cf., among others, Mt 8 : 19; Mk 4 : 38; 9 : 38; 10 : 35; 13 : 1; Jn 11 : 28.
[22] Mt 12 : 38.
[23] Lk 10 : 25; cf. Mt 22 : 16.
[24] Jn 13 : 13-14; cf. also Mt 10 : 25; 26 : 18 and parallel passages.
[25] Mt 23 : 8. Saint Ignatius of Antioch takes up this affirmation and comments as follows: "We have received the faith;

people of every kind, race and nation have for two thousand years in all the languages of the earth given him this title with veneration, repeating in their own ways the exclamation of Nicodemus: "We know that you are a teacher come from God".[26]

This image of Christ the Teacher is at once majestic and familiar, impressive and reassuring. It comes from the pen of the evangelists and it has often been evoked subsequently in iconography since earliest Christian times,[27] so captivating is it. And I am pleased to evoke it in my turn at the beginning of these considerations on catechesis in the modern world.

Teaching through his life as a whole

9.   In doing so, I am not forgetful that the majesty of Christ the Teacher and the unique consistency and persuasiveness of his teaching can only be explained by the fact that his words, his parables and his arguments are never separable from his life and his very being. Accordingly, the whole of Christ's life was a continual teaching: his silences, his miracles, his gestures, his

this is why we hold fast, in order to be recognized as disciples of Jesus Christ, our only Teacher" (*Epistola ad Magnesios,* IX, 2, FUNK 1, 198).

[26] *Jn* 3:2.

[27] The portrayal of Christ as Teacher goes back as far as the Roman Catacombs. It is frequently used in the mosaics of Romano-Byzantine art of the third and fourth centuries. It was to form a predominant artistic motif in the sculptures of the great Romanesque and Gothic cathedrals of the Middle Ages.

13

prayer, his love for people, his special affection for the little and the poor, his acceptance of the total sacrifice on the Cross for the redemption of the world, and his Resurrection are the actualization of his word and the fulfilment of revelation. Hence for Christians the crucifix is one of the most sublime and popular images of Christ the Teacher.

These consideration follow in the wake of the great traditions of the Church and they all strengthen our fervour with regard to Christ, the Teacher who reveals God to man and man to himself, the Teacher who saves, sanctifies and guides, who lives, who speaks, rouses, moves, redresses, judges, forgives, and goes with us day by day on the path of history, the Teacher who comes and will come in glory.

Only in deep communion with him will catechists find light and strength for an authentic, desirable renewal of catechesis.

II

AN EXPERIENCE AS OLD AS THE CHURCH

**The Mission
of the Apostles**

10.   The image of Christ the Teacher was stamped on the spirit of the Twelve and of the first disciples, and the command "Go ... and make disciples of all nations" [28] set the course for the whole of their lives. Saint John bears witness to this in his Gospel when he reports the words of Jesus: "No longer do I call you servants, for the servant does not know what his master is doing; but I have called you friends, for all that I have heard from my Father I have made known to you".[29]   It was not they who chose to follow Jesus; it was Jesus who chose them, kept them with him, and appointed them even before his Passover, that they should go and bear fruit and that their fruit should remain.[30] For this reason he formally conferred on them after the Resurrection the mission of making disciples of all nations.

[28] *Mt* 28 : 19.
[29] *Jn* 15 : 15.
[30] Cf. *Jn* 15 : 16.

15

The whole of the book of the Acts of the Apostles is a witness that they were faithful to their vocation and to the mission they had received. The members of the first Christian community are seen in it as "devoted to the apostles' teaching and fellowship, to the breaking of bread and the prayers".[31] Without any doubt we find in that a lasting image of the Church being born of and continually nourished by the word of the Lord, thanks to the teaching of the Apostles, celebrating that word in the Eucharistic Sacrifice and bearing witness to it before the world in the sign of charity.

When those who opposed the Apostles took offence at their activity, it was because they were "annoyed because (the Apostles) were teaching the people"[32] and the order they gave them was not to teach at all in the name of Jesus.[33] But we know that the Apostles considered it right to listen to God rather than to men on this very matter.[34]

**Catechesis
in the apostolic age**

11.   The Apostles were not slow to share with others the ministry of apostleship.[35] They transmitted to their successors the task of teaching. They entrusted it also to the deacons from

[31] *Acts* 2 :42.
[32] *Acts* 4 :2.
[33] Cf. *Acts* 4 :18; 5 :28.
[34] Cf. *Acts* 4 :19.
[35] Cf. *Acts* 1 :25.

16

the moment of their institution: Stephen, "full of grace and power", taught unceasingly, moved by the wisdom of the Spirit.[36] The Apostles associated "many others" with themselves in the task of teaching,[37] and even simple Christians scattered by persecution "went about preaching the word".[38] Saint Paul was in a pre-eminent way the herald of this preaching, from Antioch to Rome, where the last picture of him that we have in Acts is that of a person "teaching about the Lord Jesus Christ quite openly".[39] His numerous letters continue and give greater depth to his teaching. The letters of Peter, John, James and Jude are also, in every case, evidence of catechesis in the apostolic age.

Before being written down, the Gospels were the expression of an oral teaching passed on to the Christian communities, and they display with varying degrees of clarity a catechetical structure. Saint Matthew's account has indeed been called the catechist's gospel, and Saint Mark's the catechumen's gospel.

The Fathers of the Church

12. This mission of teaching that belonged to the Apostles and their first fellow workers was continued by the Church. Making herself day after day a disciple of the Lord, she earned the

---

[36] Cf. *Acts* 6 : 8 ff.; cf. also Philip catechizing the minister of the Queen of the Ethiopians: *Acts* 8: 26 ff.
[37] Cf. *Acts* 15 : 35.
[38] *Acts* 8 : 4.
[39] *Acts* 28 : 31.

title of "Mother and Teacher".[40] From Clement of Rome to Origen,[41] the post-apostolic age saw the birth of remarkable works. Next we see a striking fact: some of the most impressive Bishops and pastors, especially in the third and fourth centuries, considered it an important part of their episcopal ministry to deliver catechetical instructions and write treatises. It was the age of Cyril of Jerusalem and John Chrysostom, of Ambrose and Augustine, the age that saw the flowering, from the pen of numerous Fathers of the Church, of works that are still models for us.

It would be impossible here to recall, even very briefly, the catechesis that gave support to the spread and advance of the Church in the various periods of history, in every continent, and in the widest variety of social and cultural contexts. There was indeed no lack of difficulties. But the word of the Lord completed its course down the centuries; it sped on and triumphed, to use the words of the Apostle Paul.[42]

---

[40] Cf. Pope JOHN XXIII, Encyclical *Mater et Magistra* (*AAS* 53 [1961], p. 401): the Church is "mother" because by baptism she unceasingly begets new children and increases God's family; she is "teacher" because she makes her children grow in the grace of their baptism by nourishing their *sensus fidei* through instruction in the truths of faith.

[41] Cf., for example, the letter of Clement of Rome to the Church of Corinth, the *Didache,* the *Epistola Apostolorum,* the writings of Irenaeus of Lyons (*Demonstratio Apostolicae Praedicationis* and *Adversus Haereses*), of Tertullian (*De Baptismo*), of Clement of Alexandria (*Paedagogus*), of Cyprian (*Testimonia ad Quirinum*), of Origen (*Contra Celsum*), etc.

[42] Cf. 2 *Thess* 3 : 1.

18

13.   The ministry of catechesis draws ever fresh
energy from the Councils. The Council of Trent
is a noteworthy example of this.   It gave catechesis priority in its constitutions and decrees.
It lies at the origin of the Roman Catechism,
which is also known by the name of that Council
and which is a work of the first rank as a summary of Christian teaching and traditional theology for use by priests. It gave rise to a remarkable organization of catechesis in the Church.
It aroused the clergy to their duty of giving
catechetical instruction. Thanks to the work of
holy theologians such as Saint Charles Borromeo,
Saint Robert Bellarmine and Saint Peter Cani-
sius, it involved the publication of catechisms
that were real models for that period. May the
Second Vatican Council stir up in our time a like
enthusiasm and similar activity.

The missions are also a special area for the
application of catechesis. The people of God
have thus continued for almost two thousand
years to educate themselves in the faith in ways
adapted to the various situations of believers
and the many different circumstances in which
the Church finds herself.

Catechesis is intimately bound up with the
whole of the Church's life. Not only her geo-
graphical extension and numerical increase but
even more her inner growth and correspondence
with God's plan depend essentially on catechesis.

It is worthwhile pointing out some of the many lessons to be drawn from the experiences in Church history that we have just recalled.

Catechesis
as the Church's right and duty

14.   To begin with, it is clear that the Church has always looked on catechesis as a sacred duty and an inalienable right. On the one hand, it is certainly a duty springing from a command given by the Lord and resting above all on those who in the New Covenant receive the call to the ministry of being pastors. On the other hand, one can likewise speak of a right: from the theological point of view every baptized person, precisely by reason of being baptized, has the right to receive from the Church instruction and education enabling him or her to enter on a truly Christian life; and from the viewpoint of human rights, every human being has the right to seek religious truth and adhere to it freely, that is to say "without coercion on the part of individuals or of social groups and any human power", in such a way that in this matter of religion, "no one is to be forced to act against his or her conscience or prevented from acting in conformity to it ".[43]

That is why catechetical activity should be able to be carried out in favourable circumstances

[43] Second Vatican Council, Declaration on Religious Liberty *Dignitatis Humanae*, 2: *AAS* 58 (1966), p. 930.

of time and place, and should have access to the
mass media and suitable equipment, without
discrimination against parents, those receiving
catechesis or those imparting it. At present this
right is admittedly being given growing recogni-
tion, at least on the level of its main principles,
as is shown by international declarations and con-
ventions in which, whatever their limitations,
one can recognize the desires of the consciences
of many people today.[44] But the right is being
violated by many States, even to the point that
imparting catechesis, having it imparted, and
receiving it become punishable offences. I
vigorously raise my voice in union with the Synod
Fathers against all discrimination in the field of
catechesis, and at the same time I again make a
pressing appeal to those in authority to put a
complete end to these constraints on human freedom in general and on religious freedom in
particular.

Priority of this task

15.   The second lesson concerns the place of
catechesis in the Church's pastoral programmes.
The more the Church, whether on the local or the
universal level, gives catechesis priority over other
works and undertakings the results of which

---

[44] Cf. The Universal Declaration of Human Rights (UNO),
10 December 1948, art. 18; The International Pact on Civil and
Political Rights (UNO), 16 December 1966, art. 4; Final Act
of the Conference on European Security and Cooperation,
para. VII.

would be more spectacular, the more she finds in catechesis a strengthening of her internal life as a community of believers and of her external activity as a missionary Church. As the twentieth century draws to a close, the Church is bidden by God and by events—each of them a call from him—to renew her trust in catechetical activity as a prime aspect of her mission. She is bidden to offer catechesis her best resources in people and energy, without sparing effort, toil or material means, in order to organize it better and to train qualified personnel. This is no mere human calculation; it is an attitude of faith. And an attitude of faith always has reference to the faithfulness of God, who never fails to respond.

Shared but differentiated responsibility

16.   The third lesson is that catechesis always has been and always will be a work for which the whole Church must feel responsible and must wish to be responsible. But the Church's members have different responsibilities, derived from each one's mission. Because of their charge, pastors have, at differing levels, the chief responsibility for fostering, guiding and coordinating catechesis. For his part, the Pope has a lively awareness of the primary responsibility that rests on him in this field: in this he finds reasons for pastoral concern but principally a source of joy and hope. Priests and religious have in cate-

chesis a pre-eminent field for their apostolate. On another level, parents have a unique responsibility. Teachers, the various ministers of the Church, catechists, and also organizers of social communications, all have in various degrees very precise responsibilities in this education of the believing conscience, an education that is important for the life of the Church and affects the life of society as such. It would be one of the best results of the General Assembly of the Synod that was entirely devoted to catechesis if it stirred up in the Church as a whole and in each sector of the Church a lively and active awareness of this differentiated but shared responsibility.

Continual balanced renewal

17.   Finally, catechesis needs to be continually renewed by a certain broadening of its concept, by the revision of its methods, by the search for suitable language, and by the utilization of new means of transmitting the message. Renewal is sometimes unequal in value; the Synod Fathers realistically recognized not only an undeniable advance in the vitality of catechetical activity and promising initiatives but also the limitations or even "deficiencies" in what has been achieved to date.[45] These limitations are particularly se-

---

[45] Cf. *Synodus Episcoporum, De catechesi hoc nostro tempore tradenda praesertim pueris atque iuvenibus, Ad Populum Dei Nuntius,* 1: *loc. cit.,* pp. 3-4; cf. "L'Osservatore Romano", 30 October 1977, p. 3.

23

rious when they endanger integrity of content. The Message to the People of God rightly stressed that "routine, with its refusal to accept any change, and improvisation, with its readiness for any venture, are equally dangerous" for catechesis.[46] Routine leads to stagnation, lethargy and eventual paralysis. Improvisation begets confusion on the part of those being given catechesis and, when these are children, on the part of their parents; it also begets all kinds of deviations, and the fracturing and eventually the complete destruction of unity. It is important for the Church to give proof today, as she has done at other periods of her history, of evangelical wisdom, courage and fidelity in seeking out and putting into operation new methods and new prospects for catechetical instruction.

[46] *Ibid.*, 6: *loc. cit.*, pp. 7-8.

III

CATECHESIS
IN THE CHURCH'S PASTORAL
AND MISSIONARY ACTIVITY

**Catechesis
as a stage in evangelization**

18.   Catechesis cannot be dissociated from the Church's pastoral and missionary activity as a whole. Nevertheless it has a specific character which was repeatedly the object of inquiry during the preparatory work and throughout the course of the Fourth General Assembly of the Synod of Bishops. The question also interests the public both within and outside the Church.

This is not the place for giving a rigorous formal definition of catechesis, which has been sufficiently explained in the General Catechetical Directory.[47] It is for specialists to clarify more and more its concept and divisions.

In view of uncertainties in practice, let us simply recall the essential landmarks—they are already solidly established in Church documents—

---

[47] Sacred Congregation for the Clergy, *Directorium Catechisticum Generale,* 17-35: *AAS* 64 (1972), pp. 110-118.

that are essential for an exact understanding of catechesis and without which there is a risk of failing to grasp its full meaning and import.

All in all, it can be taken here that catechesis is an education of children, young people and adults in the faith, which includes especially the teaching of Christian doctrine imparted, generally speaking, in an organic and systematic way, with a view to initiating the hearers into the fullness of Christian life. Accordingly, while not being formally identified with them, catechesis is built on a certain number of elements of the Church's pastoral mission that have a catechetical aspect, that prepare for catechesis, or that spring from it. These elements are: the initial proclamation of the Gospel or missionary preaching through the kerygma to arouse faith, apologetics or examination of the reasons for belief, experience of Christian living, celebration of the sacraments, integration into the ecclesial community, and apostolic and missionary witness.

Let us first of all recall that there is no separation or opposition between catechesis and evangelization. Nor can the two be simply identified with each other. Instead, they have close links whereby they integrate and complement each other.

The Apostolic Exhortation *Evangelii Nuntiandi* of 8 December 1975, on evangelization in the modern world, rightly stressed that evangelization—which has the aim of bringing the Good News to the whole of humanity, so that all may live by it—is a rich, complex and dynamic reality, made up of elements, or one could say moments, that are essential and different from each other, and that must all be kept in view simultaneously.[48] Catechesis is one of these moments—a very remarkable one—in the whole process of evangelization.

**Catechesis
and the initial proclamation
of the Gospel**

19.   The specific character of catechesis, as distinct from the initial conversion-bringing proclamation of the Gospel, has the twofold objective of maturing the initial faith and of educating the true disciple of Christ by means of a deeper and more systematic knowledge of the person and the message of our Lord Jesus Christ.[49]

But in catechetical practice, this model order must allow for the fact that the initial evangelization has often not taken place. A certain number of children baptized in infancy come for catechesis in the parish without receiving any other initiation into the faith and still without any explicit personal attachment to Jesus Christ; they only have the capacity to believe placed within them by baptism and the presence of the Holy Spirit; and opposition is quickly created by the prej-

---

[48] Cf. 17-24: *AAS* 68 (1976), pp. 17-22.
[49] Cf. *Synodus Episcoporum, De catechesi hoc nostro tempore tradenda praesertim pueris atque iuvenibus, Ad Populum Dei Nuntius,* 1: *loc. cit.,* pp. 3-4; cf. "L'Osservatore Romano", 30 October 1977, p. 3.

udices of their non-Christian family background or of the positivist spirit of their education. In addition, there are other children who have not been baptized and whose parents agree only at a later date to religious education: for practical reasons, the catechumenal stage of these children will often be carried out largely in the course of the ordinary catechesis. Again, many pre-adolescents and adolescents who have been baptized and been given a systematic catechesis and the sacraments still remain hesitant for a long time about committing their whole lives to Jesus Christ, even though they do not actually try to avoid religious instruction in the name of their freedom. Finally, even adults are not safe from temptations to doubt or to abandon their faith, especially as a result of their unbelieving surroundings. This means that "catechesis" must often concern itself not only with nourishing and teaching the faith but also with arousing it unceasingly with the help of grace, with opening the heart, with converting, and with preparing total adherence to Jesus Christ on the part of those who are still on the threshold of faith. This concern will in part decide the tone, the language and the method of catechesis.

Specific aim of catechesis

20.   Nevertheless, the specific aim of catechesis is to develop, with God's help, an as yet initial faith, and to advance in fullness and to nourish day by day the Christian life of the

faithful, young and old. It is in fact a matter of giving growth, at the level of knowledge and in life, to the seed of faith sown by the Holy Spirit with the initial proclamation and effectively transmitted by baptism.

Catechesis aims therefore at developing understanding of the mystery of Christ in the light of God's word, so that the whole of a person's humanity is impregnated by that word. Changed by the working of grace into a new creature, the Christian thus sets himself to follow Christ and learns more and more within the Church to think like him, to judge like him, to act in conformity with his commandments, and to hope as he invites us to.

To put it more precisely: within the whole process of evangelization, the aim of catechesis is to be the teaching and maturation stage, that is to say, the period in which the Christian, having accepted by faith the person of Jesus Christ as the one Lord and having given him complete adherence by sincere conversion of heart, endeavours to know better this Jesus to whom he has entrusted himself: to know his "mystery", the Kingdom of God proclaimed by him, the requirements and promises contained in his Gospel message, and the paths that he has laid down for any one who wishes to follow him.

It is true that being a Christian means saying "yes" to Jesus Christ, but let us remember that this "yes" has two levels: it consists in surrendering to the word of God and relying on it, but it also means, at a later stage, endeavouring to know better and better the profound meaning of this word.

Need for systematic catechesis

21.   In his closing speech at the Fourth General Assembly of the Synod, Pope Paul VI rejoiced "to see how everyone drew attention to the absolute need for systematic catechesis, precisely because it is this reflective study of the Christian mystery that fundamentally distinguishes catechesis from all other ways of presenting the word of God ".[50]

In view of practical difficulties, attention must be drawn to some of the characteristics of this instruction:

— it must be systematic, not improvised but programmed to reach a precise goal;

— it must deal with essentials, without any claim to tackle all disputed questions or to transform itself into theological research or scientific exegesis;

— it must nevertheless be sufficiently complete, not stopping short at the initial proclamation of the Christian mystery such as we have in the kerygma;

— it must be an integral Christian initiation, open to all the other factors of Christian life.

---

[50] Concluding Address to the Synod, 29 October 1977: *AAS* 69 (1977), p. 634.

I am not forgetting the interest of the many different occasions for catechesis connected with personal, family, social and ecclesial life—these occasions must be utilized and I shall return to them in Chapter VI—but I am stressing the need for organic and systematic Christian instruction, because of the tendency in various quarters to minimize its importance.

Catechesis and life experience

22.   It is useless to play off orthopraxis against orthodoxy: Christianity is inseparably both. Firm and well-thought-out convictions lead to courageous and upright action; the endeavour to educate the faithful to live as disciples of Christ today calls for and facilitates a discovery in depth of the mystery of Christ in the history of salvation.

It is also quite useless to campaign for the abandonment of serious and orderly study of the message of Christ in the name of a method concentrating on life experience. "No one can arrive at the whole truth on the basis solely of some simple private experience, that is to say without an adequate explanation of the message of Christ, who is 'the way, and the truth, and the life' (*Jn* 14:6) ".[51]

Nor is any opposition to be set up between a catechesis taking life as its point of departure and a traditional, doctrinal and systematic cate-

[51] *Ibid.*

31

chesis.[52] Authentic catechesis is always an orderly and systematic initiation into the revelation that God has given of himself to humanity in Christ Jesus, a revelation stored in the depths of the Church's memory and in Sacred Scripture, and constantly communicated from one generation to the next by a living active *traditio*. This revelation is not however isolated from life or artificially juxtaposed to it. It is concerned with the ultimate meaning of life and it illumines the whole of life with the light of the Gospel, to inspire it or to question it.

That is why we can apply to catechists an expression used by the Second Vatican Council with special reference to priests: "instructors (of the human being and his life) in the faith".[53]

Catechesis and sacraments

23. Catechesis is intrinsically linked with the whole of liturgical and sacramental activity, for it is in the sacraments, especially in the Eucharist, that Christ Jesus works in fullness for the transformation of human beings.

In the early Church, the catechumenate and preparation for the sacraments of baptism and the Eucharist were the same thing. Although in the countries that have long been Christian the Church

---

[52] *Directorium Catechisticum Generale,* 40 and 46: *AAS* 64 (1972), pp. 121 and 124-125.
[53] Cf. Decree on the Ministry and Life of Priests *Presbyterorum Ordinis,* 6: *AAS* 58 (1966), p. 999.

has changed her practice in this field, the catechumenate has never been abolished; on the contrary, it is experiencing a renewal in those countries [54] and is abundantly practised in the young missionary Churches. In any case, catechesis always has reference to the sacraments. On the one hand, the catechesis that prepares for the sacraments is an eminent kind, and every form of catechesis necessarily leads to the sacraments of faith. On the other hand, authentic practice of the sacraments is bound to have a catechetical aspect. In other words, sacramental life is impoverished and very soon turns into hollow ritualism if it is not based on serious knowledge of the meaning of the sacraments, and catechesis becomes intellectualized if it fails to come alive in sacramental practice.

Catechesis and ecclesial community

24.   Finally, catechesis is closely linked with the responsible activity of the Church and of Christians in the world. A person who has given adherence to Jesus Christ by faith and is endeavouring to consolidate that faith by catechesis needs to live in communion with those who have taken the same step. Catechesis runs the risk of becoming barren if no community of faith and Christian life takes the catechumen in at a certain stage of his catechesis. That is why the ecclesial

[54] Cf. *Ordo Initiationis Christianae Adultorum.*

community at all levels has a twofold responsibility with regard to catechesis: it has the responsibility of providing for the training of its members, but it also has the responsibility of welcoming them into an environment where they can live as fully as possible what they have learned.

Catechesis is likewise open to missionary dynamism. If catechesis is done well, Christians will be eager to bear witness to their faith, to hand it on to their children, to make it known to others, and to serve the human community in every way.

Catechesis in the wide sense necessary for maturity and strength of faith

25.   Thus through catechesis the Gospel kerygma (the initial ardent proclamation by which a person is one day overwhelmed and brought to the decision to entrust himself to Jesus Christ by faith) is gradually deepened, developed in its implicit consequences, explained in language that includes an appeal to reason, and channelled towards Christian practice in the Church and the world.   All this is no less evangelical than the kerygma, in spite of what is said by certain people who consider that catechesis necessarily rationalizes, dries up and eventually kills all that is living, spontaneous and vibrant in the kerygma. The truths studied in catechesis are the same truths that touched the person's heart when he heard them for the first time.   Far from blunting

or exhausting them, the fact of knowing them better should make them even more challenging and decisive for one's life.

In the understanding expounded here, catechesis keeps the entirely pastoral perspective with which the Synod viewed it. This broad meaning of catechesis in no way contradicts but rather includes and goes beyond a narrow meaning which was once commonly given to catechesis in didactic expositions, namely the simple teaching of the formulas that express faith.

In the final analysis, catechesis is necessary both for the maturation of the faith of Christians and for their witness in the world: it is aimed at bringing Christians to "attain to the unity of the faith and of the knowledge of the Son of God, to mature manhood, to the measure of the stature of the fulness of Christ";[55] it is also aimed at making them prepared to make a defence to any one who calls them to account for the hope that is in them.[56]

[55] *Eph* 4:13.
[56] Cf. *1 Pt* 3:15.

IV

THE WHOLE OF THE GOOD NEWS DRAWN FROM ITS SOURCE

Content of the Message

26.   Since catechesis is a moment or aspect of evangelization, its content cannot be anything else but the content of evangelization as a whole. The one message—the Good News of salvation—that has been heard once or hundreds of times and has been accepted with the heart, is in catechesis probed unceasingly by reflection and systematic study, by awareness of its repercussions on one's personal life—an awareness calling for ever greater commitment—and by inserting it into an organic and harmonious whole, namely Christian living in society and the world.

The source

27.   Catechesis will always draw its content from the living source of the word of God transmitted in Tradition and the Scriptures, for "sacred Tradition and sacred Scripture make up a single sacred deposit of the word of God, which is entrusted to the Church", as was recalled by

the Second Vatican Council, which desired that "the ministry of the word—pastoral preaching, catechetics and all forms of Christian instruction ...—(should be) healthily nourished and (should) thrive in holiness through the word of Scripture".[57]

To speak of Tradition and Scripture as the source of catechesis is to draw attention to the fact that catechesis must be impregnated and penetrated by the thought, the spirit and the outlook of the Bible and the Gospels through assiduous contact with the texts themselves; but it is also a reminder that catechesis will be all the richer and more effective for reading the texts with the intelligence and the heart of the Church and for drawing inspiration from the two thousand years of the Church's reflection and life.

The Church's teaching, liturgy and life spring from this source and lead back to it, under the guidance of the pastors and, in particular, of the doctrinal Magisterium entrusted to them by the Lord.

The Creed
an exceptionally important expression
of doctrine

28.   An exceptionally important expression of the living heritage placed in the custody of the pastors is found in the Creed or, to put it more

---

[57] Dogmatic Constitution on Divine Revelation *Dei Verbum,* 10 and 24: *AAS* 58 (1966), pp. 822 and 828-829; cf. also Sacred Congregation for the Clergy, *Directorium Catechisticum Generale,* 45 (*AAS* 64 [1972], p. 124), where the principal and complementary sources of catechesis are well set out.

concretely, in the Creeds that at crucial moments have summed up the Church's faith in felicitous syntheses. In the course of the centuries an important element of catechesis was constituted by the *traditio Symboli* (transmission of the summary of the faith), followed by the transmission of the Lord's Prayer. This expressive rite has in our time been reintroduced into the initiation of catechumens.[58] Should not greater use be made of an adapted form of it to mark that most important stage at which a new disciple of Jesus Christ accepts with full awareness and courage the content of what will from then on be the object of his earnest study?

In the Creed of the People of God, proclaimed at the close of the nineteenth centenary of the martyrdom of the Apostles Peter and Paul, my predecessor Paul VI decided to bring together the essential elements of the Catholic faith, especially those that presented greater difficulty or risked being ignored.[59] This is a sure point of reference for the content of catechesis.

---

[58] Cf. *Ordo Initiationis Christianae Adultorum,* 25-26; 183-187.

[59] Cf. *AAS* 60 (1968), pp. 436-445. Besides these great professions of faith of the Magisterium, note also the popular professions of faith, rooted in the traditional Christian culture of certain countries; cf. what I said to the young people at Gniezno, 3 June 1979, regarding the Bogurodzica song-message: "This is not only a song: it is also a profession of faith, a symbol of the Polish Credo, it is a catechesis and also a document of Christian education. The principal truths of faith and the principles of morality are contained here. This is not only a historical object. It is a document of life. (It has even been called) 'the Polish catechism' " (*AAS* 71 [1979], p. 754).

29. In the third chapter of his Apostolic Exhortation *Evangelii Nuntiandi,* the same Pope recalled "the essential content, the living substance" of evangelization.[60] Catechesis too must keep in mind each of these factors and also the living synthesis of which they are part.[61]

I shall therefore limit myself here simply to recalling one or two points.[62] Anyone can see, for instance, how important it is to make the child, the adolescent, the person advancing in faith understand "what can be known about God";[63] to be able in a way to tell them: "What you worship as unknown, this I proclaim to you";[64] to set forth briefly for them[65] the mystery of the Word of God become man and accomplishing man's salvation by his Passover, that is to say through his death and Resurrection, but also by his preaching, by the signs worked by him, and by the sacraments of his permanent presence in our midst. The Synod Fathers were indeed inspired when they asked that care should be taken not to reduce Christ to his humanity

---

[60] 25: *AAS* 68 (1976), p. 23.

[61] *Ibid.,* especially 26-39: *l. c.,* pp. 23-25; the "principal elements of the Christian message" are presented in a more systematic fashion in the *Directorium Catechisticum Generale,* 47-69 (*AAS* 64 [1972], pp. 125-141), where one also finds the norm for the essential doctrinal content of catechesis.

[62] Consult also on this point the *Directorium Catechisticum Generale,* 37-46 (*l. c.,* pp. 120-125).

[63] *Rom* 1 : 19.

[64] *Acts* 17 : 23.

[65] Cf. *Eph* 3 : 3.

alone or his message to a no more than earthly dimension, but that he should be recognized as the Son of God, the mediator giving us in the Spirit free access to the Father.[66]

It is important to display before the eyes of the intelligence and of the heart, in the light of faith, the sacrament of Christ's presence constituted by the mystery of the Church, which is an assembly of human beings who are sinners and yet have at the same time been sanctified and who make up the family of God gathered together by the Lord under the guidance of those whom "the Holy Spirit has made ... guardians, to feed the Church of God".[67]

It is important to explain that the history of the human race, marked as it is by grace and sin, greatness and misery, is taken up by God in his Son Jesus, "foreshadowing in some way the age which is to come".[68]

Finally, it is important to reveal frankly the demands—demands that involve self-denial but also joy—made by what the Apostle Paul liked to call "newness of life",[69] "a new creation",[70] being in Christ,[71] and "eternal life in Christ Jesus",[72] which is the same thing as life in the

[66] Cf. *Eph* 2 :18.
[67] *Acts* 20 :28.
[68] Second Vatican Council, Pastoral Constitution on the Church in the Modern World *Gaudium et Spes,* 39: *AAS* 58 (1966), pp. 1056-1057.
[69] *Rom* 6 :4.
[70] *2 Cor* 5 :17.
[71] Cf. *ibid.*
[72] *Rom* 6 :23.

world but lived in accordance with the beatitudes and called to an extension and transfiguration hereafter.

Hence the importance in catechesis of personal moral commitments in keeping with the Gospel and of Christian attitudes, whether heroic or very simple, to life and the world—what we call the Christian or evangelical virtues. Hence also, in its endeavour to educate faith, the concern of catechesis not to omit but to clarify properly realities such as man's activity for his integral liberation,[73] the search for a society with greater solidarity and fraternity, the fight for justice and the building of peace.

Besides, it is not to be thought that this dimension of catechesis is altogether new. As early as the patristic age, Saint Ambrose and Saint John Chrysostom—to quote only them—gave prominence to the social consequences of the demands made by the Gospel. Close to our own time, the catechism of Saint Pius X explicitly listed oppressing the poor and depriving workers of their just wages among the sins that cry to God for vengeance.[74] Since *Rerum Novarum* especially, social concern has been actively present in the catechetical teaching of the Popes and the bishops. Many Synod Fathers rightly insisted that the rich heritage of the Church's social

[73] Cf. Pope PAUL VI, Apostolic Exhortation *Evangelii Nuntiandi*, 30-38: *AAS* 68 (1976), pp. 25-30.
[74] Cf. *Catechismo maggiore*, Fifth part, chap. 6, 965-966.

teaching should, in appropriate forms, find a place in the general catechetical education of the faithful.

Integrity of content

30.   With regard to the content of catechesis, three important points deserve special attention today.

The first point concerns the integrity of the content. In order that the sacrificial offering of his or her faith [75] should be perfect, the person who becomes a disciple of Christ has the right to receive "the word of faith" [76] not in mutilated, falsified or diminished form but whole and entire, in all its rigour and vigour. Unfaithfulness on some point to the integrity of the message means a dangerous weakening of catechesis and putting at risk the results that Christ and the ecclesial community have a right to expect from it. It is certainly not by chance that the final command of Jesus in Matthew's Gospel bears the mark of a certain entireness: "All authority ... has been given to me ... make disciples of all nations ... teaching them to observe all ... I am with you always". This is why, when a person first becomes aware of "the surpassing worth of knowing Christ Jesus",[77] whom he has encountered by faith, and has the perhaps unconscious

[75] Cf. *Phil* 2 : 17.
[76] *Rom* 10 : 8.
[77] *Phil* 3 : 8.

desire to know him more extensively and better, "hearing about him and being taught in him, as the truth is in Jesus",[78] there is no valid pretext for refusing him any part whatever of that knowledge. What kind of catechesis would it be that failed to give their full place to man's creation and sin, to God's plan of redemption and its long, loving preparation and realization, to the Incarnation of the Son of God, to Mary, the Immaculate One, the Mother of God, ever Virgin, raised body and soul to the glory of heaven, and to her role in the mystery of salvation, to the mystery of lawlessness at work in our lives [79] and the power of God freeing us from it, to the need for penance and asceticism, to the sacramental and liturgical actions, to the reality of the Eucharistic presence, to participation in divine life here and hereafter, and so on? Thus, no true catechist can lawfully, on his own initiative, make a selection of what he considers important in the deposit of faith as opposed to what he considers unimportant, so as to teach the one and reject the other.

**By means
of suitable pedagogical methods**

31.   This gives rise to a second remark. It can happen that in the present situation of catechesis reasons of method or pedagogy suggest that the communication of the riches of the

[78] Cf. *Eph* 4 : 20-21.
[79] Cf. *2 Thess* 2 : 7.

content of catechesis should be organized in one way rather than another. Besides, integrity does not dispense from balance and from the organic hierarchical character through which the truths to be taught, the norms to be transmitted, and the ways of Christian life to be indicated will be given the proper importance due to each. It can also happen that a particular sort of language proves preferable for transmitting this content to a particular individual or group. The choice made will be a valid one to the extent that, far from being dictated by more or less subjective theories or prejudices stamped with a certain ideology, it is inspired by the humble concern to stay closer to a content that must remain intact. The method and language used must truly be means for communicating the whole and not just a part of "the words of eternal life" [80] and "the ways of life".[81]

Ecumenical dimension of catechesis

32.   The great movement, one certainly inspired by the Spirit of Jesus, that has for some years been causing the Catholic Church to seek with other Christian Churches or confessions the restoration of the perfect unity willed by the Lord, brings me to the question of the ecumenical character of catechesis. This movement reached its full prominence in the Second Vatican Coun-

[80] *Jn* 6 :69; cf. *Acts* 5 :20; 7 :38.
[81] *Acts* 2 :28, quoting *Ps* 16 :11.

44

cil [82] and since then has taken on a new extension within the Church, as is shown concretely by the impressive series of events and initiatives with which everyone is now familiar.

Catechesis cannot remain aloof from this ecumenical dimension, since all the faithful are called to share, according to their capacity and place in the Church, in the movement towards unity. [83]

Catechesis will have an ecumenical dimension if, while not ceasing to teach that the fullness of the revealed truths and of the means of salvation instituted by Christ is found in the Catholic Church, [84] it does so with sincere respect, in words and in deeds, for the ecclesial communities that are not in perfect communion with this Church.

In this context, it is extremely important to give a correct and fair presentation of the other Churches and ecclesial communities that the Spirit of Christ does not refrain from using as means of salvation; "moreover, some, even very many, of the outstanding elements and endowments which together go to build up and give life to the Church herself, can exist outside the visible

[82] Cf. the entire Decree on Ecumenism *Unitatis Redintegratio: AAS* 57 (1965), pp. 90-112.

[83] Cf. *ibid.,* 5: *l. c.,* p. 96; cf. also Second Vatican Council, Decree on the Missionary Activity of the Church *Ad Gentes,* 15: *AAS* 58 (1966), pp. 963-965; Sacred Congregation of the Clergy, *Directorium Catechisticum Generale,* 27: *AAS* 64 (1972), p. 115.

[84] Cf. Second Vatican Council, Decree on Ecumenism *Unitatis Redintegratio,* 3-4: *AAS* 57 (1965), pp. 92-96.

boundaries of the Catholic Church".[85] Among other things, this presentation will help Catholics to have both a deeper understanding of their own faith and a better acquaintance with and esteem for their other Christian brethren, thus facilitating the shared search for the way towards full unity in the whole truth. It should also help non-Catholics to have a better knowledge and appreciation of the Catholic Church and her conviction of being the "universal help towards salvation".

Catechesis will have an ecumenical dimension if, in addition, it creates and fosters a true desire for unity. This will be true all the more if it inspires serious efforts—including the effort of self-purification in the humility and the fervour of the Spirit in order to clear the ways—with a view not to facile irenics made up of omissions and concessions on the level of doctrine, but to perfect unity, when and by what means the Lord will wish.

Finally, catechesis will have an ecumenical dimension if it tries to prepare Catholic children and young people, as well as adults, for living in contact with non-Catholics, affirming their Catholic identity while respecting the faith of others.

[85] *Ibid.*, 3: *l. c.*, pp. 93.

33.   In situations of religious plurality, the
Bishops can consider it opportune or even necessary to have certain experiences of collaboration in the field of catechesis between Catholics
and other Christians, complementing the normal
catechesis that must in any case be given to Catholics.   Such experiences have a theological foun-
dation in the elements shared by all Christians.[86]
But the communion of faith between Catholics
and other Christians is not complete and perfect;
in certain cases there are even profound diver-
gences.   Consequently, this ecumenical collaboration is by its very nature limited: it must never
mean a "reduction" to a common minimum.
Furthermore, catechesis does not consist merely
in the teaching of doctrine: it also means initiating into the whole of Christian life, bringing full
participation in the sacraments of the Church.
Therefore, where there is an experience of ecumenical collaboration in the field of catechesis,
care must be taken that the education of Catholics
in the Catholic Church should be well·ensured
in matters of doctrine and of Christian living.

During the Synod, a certain number of Bishops drew attention to what they referred to as
the increasingly frequent cases in which the civil
authority or other circumstances impose on the

---

[86] Cf. *ibid.*; cf. also Dogmatic Constitution on the Church
Lumen Gentium, 15: *AAS* 57 (1965), p. 19.

schools in some countries a common instruction in the Christian religion, with common textbooks, class periods, etc., for Catholics and non-Catholics alike. Needless to say, this is not true catechesis. But this teaching also has ecumenical importance when it presents Christian doctrine fairly and honestly. In cases where circumstances impose it, it is important that in addition a specifically Catholic catechesis should be ensured with all the greater care.

The question of textbooks dealing with the various religions

34.   At this point another observation must be made on the same lines but from a different point of view. State schools sometimes provide their pupils with books that for cultural reasons (history, morals or literature) present the various religions, including the Catholic religion. An objective presentation of historical events, of the different religions and of the various Christian confessions can make a contribution here to better mutual understanding. Care will then be taken that every effort is made to ensure that the presentation is truly objective and free from the distorting influence of ideological and political systems or of prejudices with claims to be scientific. In any case, such schoolbooks can obviously not be considered catechetical works: they lack both the witness of believers stating their faith to other believers and an understanding of the Christian mysteries and of what is specific about Catholicism, as these are understood within the faith.

V

EVERYBODY NEEDS TO BE CATECHIZED

**The importance of children
and the young**

35.   The theme designated by my predecessor
Paul VI for the Fourth General Assembly of the
Synod of Bishops was: "Catechesis in our time,
with special reference to the catechesis of children
and young people". The increase in the number
of young people is without doubt a fact charged
with hope and at the same time with anxiety for a
large part of the contemporary world. In certain
countries, especially those of the Third World,
more than half of the population is under twenty-
five or thirty years of age. This means millions and
millions of children and young people preparing
for their adult future. And there is more than
just the factor of numbers: recent events, as well
as the daily news, tell us that, although this count-
less multitude of young people is here and
there dominated by uncertainty and fear, seduced
by the escapism of indifference or drugs, or
tempted by nihilism and violence, nevertheless it
constitutes in its major part the great force that
amid many hazards is set on building the
civilization of the future.

In our pastoral care we ask ourselves: How are we to reveal Jesus Christ, God made man, to this multitude of children and young people, reveal him not just in the fascination of a first fleeting encounter but through an acquaintance, growing deeper and clearer daily, with him, his message, the plan of God that he has revealed, the call he addresses to each person, and the Kingdom that he wishes to establish in this world with the "little flock" [87] of those who believe in him, a Kingdom that will be complete only in eternity? How are we to enable them to know the meaning, the import, the fundamental requirements, the law of love, the promises and the hopes of this Kingdom?

There are many observations that could be made about the special characteristics that catechesis assumes at the different stages of life.

Infants

36.   One moment that is often decisive is the one at which the very young child receives the first elements of catechesis from its parents and the family surroundings. These elements will perhaps be no more than a simple revelation of a good and provident Father in heaven to whom the child learns to turn its heart. The very short prayers that the child learns to lisp will be the start of a loving dialogue with this hidden God whose word it will then begin to hear. I cannot

[87] *Lk* 12 : 32.

insist too strongly on this early initiation by Christian parents in which the child's faculties are integrated into a living relationship with God. It is a work of prime importance. It demands great love and profound respect for the child who has a right to a simple and true presentation of the Christian faith.

Children

37.   For the child there comes soon, at school and in church, in institutions connected with the parish or with the spiritual care of the Catholic or State school not only an introduction into a wider social circle, but also the moment for a catechesis aimed at inserting him or her organically into the life of the Church, a moment that includes an immediate preparation for the celebration of the sacraments. This catechesis is didactic in character, but is directed towards the giving of witness in the faith. It is an initial catechesis but not a fragmentary one, since it will have to reveal, although in an elementary way, all the principal mysteries of faith and their effects on the child's moral and religious life. It is a catechesis that gives meaning to the sacraments, but at the same time it receives from the experience of the sacraments a living dimension that keeps it from remaining merely doctrinal, and it communicates to the child the joy of being a witness to Christ in ordinary life

38.   Next comes puberty and adolescence, with all the greatness and dangers which that age brings. It is the time of discovering oneself and one's own inner world, the time of generous plans, the time when the feeling of love awakens, with the biological impulses of sexuality, the time of the desire to be together, the time of a particularly intense joy connected with the exhilarating discovery of life. But often it is also the age of deeper questioning, of anguished or even frustrating searching, of a certain mistrust of others and dangerous introspection, and the age sometimes of the first experiences of setbacks and of disappointments. Catechesis cannot ignore these changeable aspects of this delicate period of life. A catechesis capable of leading the adolescent to reexamine his or her life and to engage in dialogue, a catechesis that does not ignore the adolescent's great questions—self-giving, belief, love and the means of expressing it constituted by sexuality—such a catechesis can be decisive. The revelation of Jesus Christ as a friend, guide and model, capable of being admired but also imitated; the revelation of his message which provides an answer to the fundamental questions; the revelation of the loving plan of Christ the Saviour as the incarnation of the only authentic love and as the possibility of uniting the human race—all this can provide the basis for genuine education in faith. Above all, the mysteries of the Passion and death of Jesus, through which,

according to Saint Paul, he merited his glorious Resurrection, can speak eloquently to the adolescent's conscience and heart and cast light on his first sufferings and on the sufferings of the world that he is discovering.

The young

39.   With youth comes the moment of the first great decisions. Although the young may enjoy the support of the members of their family and their friends, they have to rely on themselves and their own conscience and must ever more frequently and decisively assume responsibility for their destiny. Good and evil, grace and sin, life and death will more and more confront one another within them, not just as moral categories but chiefly as fundamental options which they must accept or reject lucidly, conscious of their own responsibility. It is obvious that a catechesis which denounces selfishness in the name of generosity, and which without any illusory over-simplification presents the Christian meaning of work, of the common good, of justice and charity, a catechesis on international peace and on the advancement of human dignity, on development, and on liberation, as these are presented in recent documents of the Church,[88] fittingly

---

[88] Cf., for example, Second Vatican Council, Pastoral Constitution on the Church in the Modern World *Gaudium et Spes*: *AAS* 58 (1966), pp. 1025-1120; Pope PAUL VI, Encyclical *Populorum Progressio*: *AAS* 59 (1967), pp. 257-299; Apostolic Letter *Octogesima Adveniens*: *AAS* 63 (1971), pp. 401-441; Apostolic Exhortation *Evangelii Nuntiandi*: *AAS* 68 (1976), pp. 5-76.

completes in the minds of the young the good catechesis on strictly religious realities which is never to be neglected. Catechesis then takes on considerable importance, since it is the time when the Gospel can be presented, understood and accepted as capable of giving meaning to life and thus of inspiring attitudes that would have no other explanation, such as self-sacrifice, detachment, forbearance, justice, commitment, reconciliation, a sense of the Absolute and the unseen. All these are traits that distinguish a young person from his or her companions as a disciple of Jesus Christ.

Catechesis thus prepares for the important Christian commitments of adult life. For example, it is certain that many vocations to the priesthood and religious life have their origin during a well imparted catechesis in infancy and adolescence.

From infancy until the threshold of maturity, catechesis is thus a permanent school of the faith and follows the major stages of life, like a beacon lighting the path of the child, the adolescent and the young person.

The adaptation of catechesis for young people

40.   It is reassuring to note that, during the Fourth General Assembly of the Synod and the following years, the Church has widely shared in concern about how to impart catechesis to children and young people. God grant that the attention thus aroused will long endure in the

Church's consciousness. In this way the Synod has been valuable for the whole Church by seeking to trace with the greatest possible precision the complex characteristics of present-day youth; by showing that these young persons speak a language into which the message of Jesus must be translated with patience and wisdom and without betrayal; by demonstrating that, in spite of appearances, these young people have within them, even though often in a confused way, not just a readiness or openness, but rather a real desire to know "Jesus ... who is called Christ";[89] and by indicating that if the work of catechesis is to be carried out rigorously and seriously, it is today more difficult and tiring than ever before, because of the obstacles and difficulties of all kinds that it meets; but it is also more consoling, because of the depth of the response it receives from children and young people. This is a treasure which the Church can and should count on in the years ahead.

Some categories of young people to whom catechesis is directed call for special attention because of their particular situation.

The handicapped

41. Children and young people who are physically or mentally handicapped come first to mind. They have a right, like others of their age, to know "the mystery of faith". The greater dif-

---

[89] *Mt* 1 :16.

ficulties that they encounter give greater merit to their efforts and to those of their teachers. It is pleasant to see that Catholic organizations especially dedicated to young handicapped people contributed to the Synod their experience in this matter, and drew from the Synod a renewed desire to deal better with this important problem. They deserve to be given warm encouragement in this endeavour.

Young people without religious support

42.   My thoughts turn next to the ever increasing number of children and young people born and brought up in a non-Christian or at least non-practising home but who wish to know the Christian faith. They must be ensured a catechesis attuned to them, so that they will be able to grow in faith and live by it more and more, in spite of the lack of support or even the opposition they meet in their surroundings.

Adults

43.   To continue the series of receivers of catechesis, I cannot fail to emphasize now one of the most constant concerns of the Synod Fathers, a concern imposed with vigour and urgency by present experiences throughout the world: I am referring to the central problem of the catechesis of adults. This is the principal form of catechesis, because it is addressed to persons who have the greatest responsibilities and the capacity to live the Christian message in its fully developed

form.[90] The Christian community cannot carry out a permanent catechesis without the direct and skilled participation of adults, whether as receivers or as promoters of catechetical activity. The world in which the young are called to live and gives witness to the faith which catechesis seeks to deepen and strengthen is governed by adults: the faith of these adults too should continually be enlightened, stimulated and renewed, so that it may pervade the temporal realities in their charge. Thus, for catechesis to be effective, it must be permanent, and it would be quite useless if it stopped short just at the threshold of maturity, since catechesis, admittedly under another form, proves no less necessary for adults.

Quasi-catechumens

44.   Among the adults who need catechesis, our pastoral missionary concern is directed to those who were born and reared in areas not yet Christianized, and who have never been able to study deeply the Christian teaching that the circumstances of life have at a certain moment caused them to come across. It is also directed to those who in childhood received a catechesis suited to their age but who later drifted away from all

[90] Cf. Second Vatican Council, Decree on the Bishop's Pastoral Office in the Church *Christus Dominus,* 14: *AAS* 58 (1966), p. 679; Decree on the Missionary Activity of the Church *Ad Gentes,* 14: *AAS* 58 (1966), pp. 962-963; Sacred Congregation for the Clergy, *Directorium Catechisticum Generale,* 20: *AAS* 64 (1972), p. 112; cf. also *Ordo Initiationis Christianae Adultorum.*

religious practice and as adults find themselves with religious knowledge of a rather childish kind. It is likewise directed to those who feel the effects of a catechesis received early in life but badly imparted or badly assimilated. It is directed to those who, although they were born in a Christian country or in sociologically Christian surroundings, have never been educated in their faith and, as adults, are really catechumens.

**Diversified
and complementary forms
of catechesis**

45.   Catechesis is therefore for adults of every age, including the elderly—persons who deserve particular attention in view of their experience and their problems—no less than for children, adolescents and the young. We should also mention migrants, those who are by-passed by modern developments, those who live in areas of large cities which are often without churches, buildings and suitable organization, and other such groups. It is desirable that initiatives meant to give all these groups a Christian formation, with appropriate means (audio-visual aids, booklets, discussions, lectures), should increase in number, enabling many adults to fill the gap left by an insufficient or deficient catechesis, to complete harmoniously at a higher level their childhood catechesis, or even to prepare themselves enough in this field to be able to help others in a more serious way.

It is important also that the catechesis of children and young people, permanent catechesis, and the catechesis of adults should not be separate watertight compartments. It is even more important that there should be no break between them. On the contrary, their perfect complementarity must be fostered: adults have much to give to young people and children in the field of catechesis, but they can also receive much from them for the growth of their own Christian lives.

It must be restated that nobody in the Church of Jesus Christ should feel excused from receiving catechesis. This is true even of young seminarians and young religious, and of all those called to the task of being pastors and catechists. They will fulfil this task all the better if they are humble pupils of the Church, the great giver as well as the great receiver of catechesis.

VI

SOME WAYS AND MEANS
OF CATECHESIS

Communications media

46.   From the oral teaching by the Apostles
and the letters circulating among the Churches
down to the most modern means, catechesis has
not ceased to look for the most suitable ways
and means for its mission, with the active participation of the communities and at the urging
of the pastors. This effort must continue.

I think immediately of the great possibilities
offered by the means of social communication and
the means of group communication: television,
radio, the press, records, tape-recordings — the
whole series of audio-visual means. The achieve-
ments in these spheres are such as to encourage
the greatest hope. Experience shows, for example,
the effect had by instruction given on radio or
television, when it combines a high aesthetic level
and rigorous fidelity to the Magisterium.   The
Church now has many opportunities for consider-
ing these questions—as, for instance, on Social
Communications Days—and it is not necessary
to speak of them at length here, in spite of their
prime importance.

60

47.   I am also thinking of various occasions of special value which are exactly suitable for catechesis: for example, diocesan, regional or national pilgrimages, which gain from being centred on some judiciously chosen theme based on the life of Christ, of the Blessed Virgin or of the Saints. Then there are the traditional missions, often too hastily dropped but irreplaceable for the periodic and vigorous renewal of Christian life—they should be revived and brought up to date. Again, there are Bible-study groups, which ought to go beyond exegesis and lead their members to live by the word of God.   Yet other instances are the meetings of ecclesial basic communities, insofar as they correspond to the criteria laid down in the Apostolic Exhortation *Evangelii Nuntiandi.*[91]   I may also mention the youth groups that, under varying names and forms but always with the purpose of making Jesus Christ known and of living by the Gospel, are in some areas multiplying and flourishing in a sort of springtime that is very comforting for the Church: these include Catholic Action groups, charitable groups, prayer groups and Christian meditation groups.   These groups are a source of great hope for the Church of tomorrow.   But, in the name of Jesus, I exhort the young people who belong to them, their leaders, and the priests who devote the best part

[91] Cf. 58: *AAS* 68 (1976), pp. 46-49.

of their ministry to them: No matter what it costs, do not allow these groups—which are exceptional occasions for meeting others, and which are blessed with such riches of friendship and solidarity among the young, of joy and enthusiasm, of reflection on events and facts—do not allow them to lack serious study of Christian doctrine. If they do, they will be in danger—a danger that has unfortunately proved only too real—of disappointing their members and also the Church.

The catechetical endeavour that is possible in these various surroundings, and in many others besides, will have all the greater chance of being accepted and bearing fruit if it respects their individual nature. By becoming part of them in the right way, it will achieve the diversity and complementarity of approach that will enable it to develop all the riches of its concept, with its three dimensions of word, memorial and witness —doctrine, celebration and commitment in living—which the Synod message to the People of God emphasized.[92]

The homily

48.   This remark is even more valid for the catechesis given in the setting of the liturgy, especially at the Eucharistic assembly. Respecting the specific nature and proper cadence of

---

[92] Cf. *Synodus Episcoporum, De catechesi hoc nostro tempore tradenda praesertim pueris atque iuvenibus, Ad Populum Dei Nuntius*, 7-10: *loc. cit.*, pp. 9-12; cf. "L'Osservatore Romano", 30 October 1977, p. 3.

this setting, the homily takes up again the journey of faith put forward by catechesis, and brings it to its natural fulfilment. At the same time it encourages the Lord's disciples to begin anew each day their spiritual journey in truth, adoration and thanksgiving. Accordingly, one can say that catechetical teaching too finds its source and its fulfilment in the Eucharist, within the whole circle of the liturgical year. Preaching, centered upon the Bible texts, must then in its own way make it possible to familiarize the faithful with the whole of the mysteries of the faith and with the norms of Christian living. Much attention must be given to the homily: it should be neither too long nor too short; it should always be carefully prepared, rich in substance and adapted to the hearers, and reserved to ordained ministers. The homily should have its place not only in every Sunday and feast-day Eucharist, but also in the celebration of baptisms, penitential liturgies, marriages and funerals. This is one of the benefits of the liturgical renewal.

Catechetical literature

49.   Among these various ways and means—all the Church's activities have a catechetical dimension—catechetical works, far from losing their essential importance, acquire fresh significance. One of the major features of the renewal of catechetics today is the rewriting and multiplication of catechetical books taking place in many

parts of the Church. Numerous very successful works have been produced and are a real treasure in the service of catechetical instruction. But it must be humbly and honestly recognized that this rich flowering has brought with it articles and publications which are ambiguous and harmful to young people and to the life of the Church. In certain places, the desire to find the best forms of expression or to keep up with fashions in pedagogical methods has often enough resulted in certain catechetical works which bewilder the young and even adults, either by deliberately or unconsciously omitting elements essential to the Church's faith, or by attributing excessive importance to certain themes at the expense of others, or, chiefly, by a rather horizontalist overall view out of keeping with the teaching of the Church's Magisterium.

Therefore, it is not enough to multiply catechetical works. In order that these works may correspond with their aim, several conditions are essential:

a) they must be linked with the real life of the generation to which they are addressed, showing close acquaintance with its anxieties and questionings, struggles and hopes;

b) they must try to speak a language comprehensible to the generation in question;

c) they must make a point of giving the whole message of Christ and his Church, without neglecting or distorting anything, and in expounding it they will follow a line and structure that highlights what is essential;

d) they must really aim to give to those who use them a better knowledge of the mysteries of Christ, aimed at true conversion and a life more in conformity with God's will.

Catechisms

50.   All those who take on the heavy task of preparing these catechetical tools, especially catechism texts, can do so only with the approval of the pastors who have the authority to give it, and taking their inspiration as closely as possible from the General Catechetical Directory, which remains the standard of reference.[93]

In this regard, I must warmly encourage the Episcopal Conferences of the whole world to undertake, patiently but resolutely, the considerable work to be accomplished in agreement with the Apostolic See in order to prepare genuine catechisms which will be faithful to the essential content of Revelation and up to date in method, and which will be capable of educating the Christian generations of the future to a sturdy faith.

This brief mention of ways and means of modern catechetics does not exhaust the wealth

---

[93] Cf. Sacred Congregation for the Clergy, *Directorium Catechisticum Generale,* 119-121; 134: *AAS* 64 (1972), pp. 166-167; 172.

of suggestions worked out by the Synod Fathers. It is comforting to think that at the present time every country is seeing valuable collaboration for a more organic and more secure renewal of these aspects of catechetics. There can be no doubt that the Church will find the experts and the right means for responding, with God's grace, to the complex requirements of communicating with the people of today.

VII

HOW TO IMPART CATECHESIS

Diversity of methods

51.   The age and the intellectual development of Christians, their degree of ecclesial and spiritual maturity and many other personal circumstances demand that catechesis should adopt widely differing methods for the attainment of its specific aim: education in the faith.   On a more general level, this variety is also demanded by the social and cultural surroundings in which the Church carries out her catechetical work.

The variety in the methods used is a sign of life and a resource.   That is how it was considered by the Fathers of the Fourth General Assembly of the Synod, although they also drew attention to the conditions necessary for that variety to be useful and not harmful to the unity of the teaching of the one faith.

At the service of Revelation and conversion

52.   The first question of a general kind that presents itself here concerns the danger and the temptation to mix catechetical teaching unduly with overt or masked ideological views, especially political and social ones, or with personal politi-

cal options. When such views get the better of the central message to be transmitted, to the point of obscuring it and putting it in second place or even using it to further their own ends, catechesis then becomes radically distorted. The Synod rightly insisted on the need for catechesis to remain above one-sided divergent trends—to avoid "dichotomies"—even in the field of theological interpretation of such questions. It is on the basis of Revelation that catechesis will try to set its course, Revelation as transmitted by the universal Magisterium of the Church, in its solemn or ordinary form. This Revelation tells of a creating and redeeming God, whose Son has come among us in our flesh and enters not only into each individual's personal history but into human history itself, becoming its centre. Accordingly, this Revelation tells of the radical change of man and the universe, of all that makes up the web of human life under the influence of the Good News of Jesus Christ. If conceived in this way, catechesis goes beyond every form of formalistic moralism, although it will include true Christian moral teaching. Chiefly, it goes beyond any kind of temporal, social or political "messianism". It seeks to arrive at man's innermost being.

The message embodied in cultures

53. Now a second question. As I said recently to the members of the Biblical Commission: "The term 'acculturation' or 'inculturation' may

be a neologism, but it expresses very well one factor of the great mystery of the Incarnation".[94] We can say of catechesis, as well as of evangelization in general, that it is called to bring the power of the Gospel into the very heart of culture and cultures. For this purpose, catechesis will seek to know these cultures and their essential components; it will learn their most significant expressions; it will respect their particular values and riches. In this manner it will be able to offer these cultures the knowledge of the hidden mystery[95] and help them to bring forth from their own living tradition original expressions of Christian life, celebration and thought. Two things must however be kept in mind.

On the one hand the Gospel message cannot be purely and simply isolated from the culture in which it was first inserted (the Biblical world or, more concretely, the cultural milieu in which Jesus of Nazareth lived), nor, without serious loss, from the cultures in which it has already been expressed down the centuries; it does not spring spontaneously from any cultural soil; it has always been transmitted by means of an apostolic dialogue which inevitably becomes part of a certain dialogue of cultures.

On the other hand, the power of the Gospel everywhere transforms and regenerates. When

[94] Cf. *AAS* 71 (1979), p. 607.
[95] Cf. *Rom* 16:25; *Eph* 3:5.

that power enters into a culture, it is no surprise that it rectifies many of its elements. There would be no catechesis if it were the Gospel that had to change when it came into contact with the cultures.

To forget this would simply amount to what Saint Paul very forcefully calls "emptying the cross of Christ of its power".[96]

It is a different matter to take, with wise discernment, certain elements, religious or otherwise, that form part of the cultural heritage of a human group and use them to help its members to understand better the whole of the Christian mystery. Genuine catechists know that catechesis "takes flesh" in the various cultures and milieux: one has only to think of the peoples with their great differences, of modern youth, of the great variety of circumstances in which people find themselves today. But they refuse to accept an impoverishment of catechesis through a renunciation or obscuring of its message, by adaptations, even in language, that would endanger the "precious deposit" of the faith,[97] or by concessions in matters of faith or morals. They are convinced that true catechesis eventually enriches these cultures by helping them to go beyond the defective or even inhuman features in them, and by communicating to their legitimate values the fullness of Christ.[98]

[96] *1 Cor* 1 :17.
[97] Cf. *2 Tim* 1 :14.
[98] Cf. *Jn* 1 :16; *Eph* 1 :10.

54.   Another question of method concerns the
utilization in catechetical instruction of valid
elements in popular piety. I have in mind devo-
tions practised by the faithful in certain regions
with moving fervour and purity of intention,
even if the faith underlying them needs to be
purified or rectified in many aspects. I have in
mind certain easily understood prayers that many
simple people are fond of repeating. I have in
mind certain acts of piety practised with a sincere desire to do penance or to please the Lord.
Underlying most of these prayers and practices,
besides elements that should be discarded, there
are other elements which, if they were properly
used, could serve very well to help people advance towards knowledge of the mystery of
Christ and of his message: the love and mercy
of God, the Incarnation of Christ, his redeeming
Cross and Resurrection, the activity of the Spirit
in each Christian and in the Church, the mystery
of the hereafter, the evangelical virtues to be
practised, the presence of the Christian in the
world, etc. And why should we appeal to non-
Christian or even anti-Christian elements, refusing to build on elements which, even if they
need to be revised and improved, have something
Christian at their root?

55. The final methodological question the importance of which should at least be referred to—one that was debated several times in the Synod—is that of memorization. In the beginnings of Christian catechesis, which coincided with a civilization that was mainly oral, recourse was had very freely to memorization. Catechesis has since then known a long tradition of learning the principal truths by memorizing. We are all aware that this method can present certain disadvantages, not the least of which is that it lends itself to insufficient or at times almost non-existent assimilation, reducing all knowledge to formulas that are repeated without being properly understood. These disadvantages and the different characteristics of our own civilization have in some places led to the almost complete suppression—according to some, alas, the definitive suppression—of memorization in catechesis. And yet certain very authoritative voices made themselves heard on the occasion of the Fourth General Assembly of the Synod, calling for the restoration of a judicious balance between reflection and spontaneity, between dialogue and silence, between written work and memory work. Moreover certain cultures still set great value on memorization.

At a time when, in non-religious teaching in certain countries, more and more complaints are being made about the unfortunate consequences of disregarding the human faculty of memory, should we not attempt to put this faculty back into use in an intelligent and even an original way in catechesis, all the more since the celebration or "memorial" of the great events of the history of salvation require a precise knowledge of them? A certain memorization of the words of Jesus, of important Bible passages, of the Ten Commandments, of the formulas of profession of the faith, of the liturgical texts, of the essential prayers, of key doctrinal ideas, etc., far from being opposed to the dignity of young Christians, or constituting an obstacle to personal dialogue with the Lord, is a real need, as the Synod Fathers forcefully recalled. We must be realists. The blossoms, if we way call them that, of faith and piety do not grow in the desert places of a memory-less catechesis. What is essential is that the texts that are memorized must at the same time be taken in and gradually understood in depth, in order to become a source of Christian life on the personal level and the community level.

The plurality of methods in contemporary catechesis can be a sign of vitality and ingenuity. In any case, the method chosen must ultimately be referred to a law that is fundamental for the whole of the Church's life: the law of fidelity to God and of fidelity to man in a single loving attitude.

VIII

THE JOY OF FAITH
IN A TROUBLED WORLD

Affirming Christian identity

56.   We live in a difficult world in which the anguish of seeing the best creations of man slip away from him and turn against him creates a climate of uncertainty.[99] In this world catechesis should help Christians to be, for their own joy and the service of all, "light" and "salt".[100] Undoubtedly this demands that catechesis should strengthen them in their identity and that it should continually separate itself from the surrounding atmosphere of hesitation, uncertainty and insipidity. Among the many difficulties, each of them a challenge for faith, I shall indicate a few in order to assist catechesis in overcoming them.

In an indifferent world

57.   A few years ago, there was much talk of the secularized world, the post-Christian era. Fashion changes, but a profound reality remains.

---

[99] Cf. Encyclical *Redemptor Hominis,* 15-16: *AAS* 71 (1979), pp. 286-295.
[100] Cf. *Mt* 5 : 13-16.

Christians today must be formed to live in a world which largely ignores God or which, in religious matters, in place of an exacting and fraternal dialogue, stimulating for all, too often flounders in a debasing indifferentism, if it does not remain in a scornful attitude of "suspicion" in the name of the progress it has made in the field of scientific "explanations". To "hold on" in this world, to offer to all a "dialogue of salvation" [101] in which each person feels respected in his or her most basic dignity, the dignity of one who is seeking God, we need a catechesis which trains the young people and adults of our communities to remain clear and consistent in their faith, to affirm serenely their Christian and Catholic identity, to "see him who is invisible" [102] and to adhere so firmly to the absoluteness of God that they can be witnesses to him in a materialistic civilization that denies him.

With the original pedagogy of the faith

58.   The irreducible originality of Christian identity has for corollary and condition no less original a pedagogy of the faith. Among the many prestigious sciences of man that are nowadays making immense advances, pedagogy is certainly one of the most important. The attainments of the other sciences—biology, psycho-

---

[101] Cf. Pope PAUL VI, Encyclical *Ecclesiam Suam*, Part Three. *AAS* 56 (1964), pp. 637-659.
[102] Cf. *Heb* 11 : 27.

logy, sociology—are providing it with valuable elements. The science of education and the art of teaching are continually being subjected to review, with a view to making them better adapted or more effective, with varying degrees of success.

There is also a pedagogy of faith, and the good that it can do for catechesis cannot be overstated. In fact, it is natural that techniques perfected and tested for education in general should be adapted for the service of education in the faith. However, account must always be taken of the absolute originality of faith. Pedagogy of faith is not a question of transmitting human knowledge, even of the highest kind; it is a question of communicating God's Revelation in its entirety. Throughout sacred history, especially in the Gospel, God himself used a pedagogy that must continue to be a model for the pedagogy of faith. A technique is of value in catechesis only to the extent that it serves the faith that is to be transmitted and learned; otherwise it is of no value.

Language suited to the service of the Credo

59. A problem very close to the preceding one is that of language. This is obviously a burning question today. It is paradoxical to see that, while modern studies, for instance in the field of communication, semantics and symbolology, attribute extraordinary importance to language,

nevertheless language is being misused today for ideological mystification, for mass conformity in thought and for reducing man to the level of an object.

All this has extensive influence in the field of catechesis. For catechesis has a pressing obligation to speak a language suited to today's children and young people in general and to many other categories of people—the language of students, intellectuals and scientists; the language of the illiterate or of people of simple culture; the language of the handicapped, and so on. Saint Augustine encountered this same problem and contributed to its solution for his own time with his well-known work *De Catechizandis Rudibus*. In catechesis as in theology, there is no doubt that the question of language is of the first order. But there is good reason for recalling here that catechesis cannot admit any language that would result in altering the substance of the content of the Creed, under any pretext whatever, even a pretended scientific one. Deceitful or beguiling language is no better. On the contrary, the supreme rule is that the great advances in the science of language must be capable of being placed at the service of catechesis so as to enable it really to "tell" or "communicate" to the child, the adolescent, the young people and adults of today the whole content of doctrine without distortion.

60.   A more subtle challenge occasionally comes
from the very way of conceiving faith. Certain contemporary philosophical schools, which
seem to be exercising a strong influence on some
theological currents and, through them, on pastoral practice, like to emphasize that the fundamental human attitude is that of seeking the infi-
nite, a seeking that never attains its object. In
theology, this view of things will state very cate-
gorically that faith is not certainty but questioning, not clarity but a leap in the dark.

These currents of thought certainly have the
advantage of reminding us that faith concerns
things not yet in our possession, since they are
hoped for; that as yet we see only "in a mirror
dimly";[103] and that God dwells always in inac-
cessible light.[104] They help us to make the Christian faith not the attitude of one who has already
arrived, but a journey forward as with Abraham.
For all the more reason one must avoid presenting as certain things which are not.

However, we must not fall into the opposite
extreme, as too often happens. The Letter to the
Hebrews says that "faith is the assurance of
things hoped for, the conviction of things not
seen".[105] Although we are not in full possession,
we do have an assurance and a conviction. When

---

[103] *1 Cor* 13 : 12.
[104] Cf. *1 Tim* 6 : 16.
[105] *Heb* 11 : 1.

educating children, adolescents and young people, let us not give them too negative an idea of faith—as if it were absolute non-knowing, a kind of blindness, a world of darkness—but let us show them that the humble yet courageous seeking of the believer, far from having its starting point in nothingness, in plain self-deception, in fallible opinions or in uncertainty, is based on the word of God who cannot deceive or be deceived, and is unceasingly built on the immovable rock of this word. It is the search of the Magi under the guidance of a star,[106] the search of which Pascal, taking up a phrase of Saint Augustine, wrote so profoundly: "You would not be searching for me, if you had not found me".[107]

It is also one of the aims of catechesis to give young catechumens the simple but solid certainties that will help them to seek to know the Lord more and better.

Catechesis and theology

61.   In this context, it seems important to me that the connection between catechesis and theology should be well understood.

Obviously this connection is profound and vital for those who understand the irreplaceable mission of theology in the service of faith. Thus it is no surprise that every stirring in the field

---

[106] Cf. *Mt* 2 :1 ff.
[107] BLAISE PASCAL, *Le mystère de Jésus: Pensées*, 553.

of theology also has repercussions in that of catechesis. In this period immediately after the Council, the Church is living through an important but hazardous time of theological research. The same must be said of hermeneutics with respect to exegesis.

Synod Fathers from all continents dealt with this question in very frank terms: they spoke of the danger of an "unstable balance" passing from theology to catechesis and they stressed the need to do something about this difficulty. Pope Paul VI himself had dealt with the problem in no less frank terms in the introduction to his Solemn Profession of Faith [108] and in the Apostolic Exhortation marking the fifth anniversary of the close of the Second Vatican Council.[109]

This point must again be insisted on. Aware of the influence that their research and their statements have on catechetical instruction, theologians and exegetes have a duty to take great care that people do not take for a certainty what on the contrary belongs to the area of questions of opinion or of discussion among experts. Catechists for their part must have the wisdom to pick from the field of theological research those points that can provide light for their own reflection and their teaching, drawing, like the theologians, from the true sources, in

[108] Pope PAUL VI, *Sollemnis Professio Fidei*, 4: *AAS* 60 (1968), p. 434.
[109] Pope PAUL VI, Apostolic Exhortation *Quinque Iam Anni*: *AAS* 63 (1971), p. 99.

the light of the Magisterium. They must refuse to trouble the minds of the children and young people, at this stage of their catechesis, with outlandish theories, useless questions and unproductive discussions, things that Saint Paul often condemned in his pastoral letters.[110]

The most valuable gift that the Church can offer to the bewildered and restless world of our time is to form within it Christians who are confirmed in what is essential and who are humbly joyful in their faith. Catechesis will teach this to them, and it will itself be the first to benefit from it: "The man who wishes to understand himself thoroughly—and not just in accordance with immediate, partial, often superficial, and even illusory standards and measures of his being—must come to Christ with his unrest and uncertainty, and even his weakness and sinfulness, his life and death. He must, so to speak, enter into Christ with all his own self, he must 'appropriate' Christ and assimilate the whole of the reality of the Incarnation and Redemption in order to find himself".[111]

---

[110] Cf. *1 Tim* 1 : 3 ff.; 4 : 1 ff.; *2 Tim* 2 : 14 ff.; 4 : 1-5; *Tit* 1 : 10-12; cf. also Apostolic Exhortation *Evangelii Nuntiandi,* 78: *AAS* 68 (1976), p. 70.
[111] Encyclical *Redemptor Hominis,* 10: *AAS* 71 (1979), p. 274.

IX

THE TASK CONCERNS US ALL

Encouragement to all responsible for catechesis

62.   Now, beloved Brothers and sons and daughters, I would like my words, which are intended as a serious and heartfelt exhortation from me in my ministry as pastor of the universal Church, to set your hearts aflame, like the letters of Saint Paul to his companions in the Gospel, Titus and Timothy, or like Saint Augustine writing for the deacon Deogratias, when the latter lost heart before his task as a catechist, a real little treatise on the joy of catechizing.[112] Yes, I wish to sow courage, hope and enthusiasm abundantly in the hearts of all those many diverse people who are in charge of religious instruction and training for life in keeping with the Gospel.

Bishops

63.   To begin with, I turn to my brother Bishops: The Second Vatican Council has already explicitly reminded you of your task in the cate-

---

[112] *De Catechizandis Rudibus, PL* 40, 310-347.

chetical area,[113] and the Fathers of the Fourth General Assembly of the Synod have also strongly underlined it.

Dearly beloved Brothers, you have here a special mission within your Churches: you are beyond all others the ones primarily responsible for catechesis, the catechists par excellence. Together with the Pope, in the spirit of episcopal collegiality, you too have charge of catechesis throughout the Church. Accept therefore what I say to you from my heart.

I know that your ministry as Bishops is growing daily more complex and overwhelming. A thousand duties call you: from the training of new priests to being actively present within the lay communities, from the living, worthy celebration of the sacraments and acts of worship to concern for human advancement and the defence of human rights. But let the concern to foster active and effective catechesis yield to no other care whatever in any way. This concern will lead you to transmit personally to your faithful the doctrine of life. But it should also lead you to take on in your diocese, in accordance with the plans of the Episcopal Conference to which you belong, the chief management of catechesis, while at the same time surrounding yourselves with competent and trustworthy assistants. Your principal role will be to bring about and maintain

[113] Cf. Decree on the Bishop's Pastoral Office in the Church *Christus Dominus*, 14: *AAS* 58 (1966), p. 679.

in your Churches a real passion for catechesis, a passion embodied in a pertinent and effective organization, putting into operation the necessary personnel, means and equipment, and also financial resources. You can be sure that if catechesis is done well in your local Churches, everything else will be easier to do. And needless to say, although your zeal must sometimes impose upon you the thankless task of denouncing deviations and correcting errors, it will much more often win for you the joy and consolation of seeing your Churches flourishing because catechesis is given in them as the Lord wishes.

Priests

64.   For your part, priests, here you have a field in which you are the immediate assistants of your Bishops. The Council has called you "instructors in the faith"; [114] there is no better way for you to be such instructors than by devoting your best efforts to the growth of your communities in the faith. Whether you are in charge of a parish, or are chaplains to primary or secondary schools or universities, or have responsibility for pastoral activity at any level, or are leaders of large or small communities, especially youth groups, the Church expects you to neglect nothing with a view to a well-organized and well-oriented catechetical effort. The deacons

[114] Decree on the Ministry and Life of Priests *Presbyterorum Ordinis*, 6: *AAS* 58 (1966), p. 999.

and other ministers that you may have the good
fortune to have with you are your natural assistants in this. All believers have a right to
catechesis; all pastors have the duty to provide
it. I shall always ask civil leaders to respect
the freedom of catechetical teaching; but with
all my strength I beg you, ministers of Jesus
Christ: Do not, for lack of zeal or because of
some unfortunate preconceived idea, leave the
faithful without catechesis. Let it not be said
that "the children beg for food, but no one gives
to them".[115]

Men and women religious

65. Many religious institutes for men and
women came into being for the purpose of giving
Christian education to children and young people,
especially the most abandoned. Throughout history, men and women religious have been deeply
committed to the Church's catechetical activity,
doing particularly apposite and effective work.
At a time when it is desired that the links
between religious and pastors should be accen-
tuated and consequently the active presence of
religious communities and their members in the
pastoral projects of the local Churches, I wholeheartedly exhort you whose religious consecration
should make you even more readily available for
the Church's service to prepare as well as possible for the task of catechesis according to the
differing vocations of your institutes and the mis-

[115] *Lam* 4 : 4.

sions entrusted to you, and to carry this concern everywhere. Let the communities dedicate as much as possible of what ability and means they have to the specific work of catechesis.

Lay catechists

66. I am anxious to give thanks in the Church's name to all of you, lay teachers of catechesis in the parishes, the men and the still more numerous women throughout the world, who are devoting yourselves to the religious education of many generations. Your work is often lowly and hidden but it is carried out with ardent and generous zeal, and it is an eminent form of the lay apostolate, a form that is particularly important where for various reasons children and young people do not receive suitable religious training in the home. How many of us have received from people like you our first notions of catechism and our preparation for the sacrament of penance, for our first communion and confirmation! The Fourth General Assembly of the Synod did not forget you. I join with it in encouraging you to continue your collaboration for the life of the Church.

But the term "catechists" belongs above all to the catechists in mission lands. Born of families that are already Christian or converted at some time to Christianity and instructed by missionaries or by another catechist, they then consecrate their lives, year after year, to catechizing children and adults in their own country.

Churches that are flourishing today would not have been built up without them. I rejoice at the efforts made by the Sacred Congregation for the Evangelization of Peoples to improve more and more the training of these catechists. I gratefully recall the memory of those whom the Lord has already called to himself. I beg the intercession of those whom my predecessors have raised to the glory of the altars. I wholeheartedly encourage those engaged in the work. I express the wish that many others may succeed them and that they may increase in numbers for a task so necessary for the missions.

In the parish

67.   I now wish to speak of the actual setting in which all these catechists normally work. I am returning this time, taking a more overall view, to the "places" for catechesis, some of which have already been mentioned in Chapter VI: the parish, the family, the school, organizations.

It is true that catechesis can be given anywhere, but I wish to stress, in accordance with the desire of very many Bishops, that the parish community must continue to be the prime mover and pre-eminent place for catechesis. Admittedly, in many countries the parish has been as it were shaken by the phenomenon of urbanization. Perhaps some have too easily accepted that the parish should be considered old-fashioned, if not doomed to disappear, in favour of more pertinent and effective small communities. Whatever

87

one may think, the parish is still a major point of reference for the Christian people, even for the non-practising. Accordingly, realism and wisdom demand that we continue along the path aiming to restore to the parish, as needed, more adequate structures and, above all, a new impetus through the increasing integration into it of qualified, responsible and generous members. This being said, and taking into account the necessary diversity of places for catechesis (the parish as such, families taking in children and adolescents, chaplaincies for State schools, Catholic educational establishments, apostolic movements that give periods of catechesis, clubs open to youth in general, spiritual formation weekends, etc.), it is supremely important that all these catechetical channels should really converge on the same confession of faith, on the same membership of the Church, and on commitments in society lived in the same Gospel spirit: "one Lord, one faith, one baptism, one God and Father".[116] That is why every big parish or every group of parishes with small numbers has the serious duty to train people completely dedicated to providing catechetical leadership (priests, men and women religious, and lay people), to provide the equipment needed for catechesis under all aspects, to increase and adapt the places for catechesis to the extent that it is possible and useful to do so, and to be watchful about the quality of the

[116] *Eph* 4 :5-6.

religious formation of the various groups and their integration into the ecclesial community.

In short, without monopolizing or enforcing uniformity, the parish remains, as I have said, the pre-eminent place for catechesis. It must rediscover its vocation, which is to be a fraternal and welcoming family home, where those who have been baptized and confirmed become aware of forming the People of God. In that home, the bread of good doctrine and the Eucharistic Bread are broken for them in abundance, in the setting of the one act of worship; [117] from that home they are sent out day by day to their apostolic mission in all the centres of activity of the life of the world.

In the family

68. The family's catechetical activity has a special character, which is in a sense irreplaceable. This special character has been rightly stressed by the Church, particularly by the Second Vatican Council.[118] Education in the faith by parents,

---

[117] Cf. Second Vatican Council, Constitution on the Sacred Liturgy *Sacrosanctum Concilium,* 35, 52: *AAS* 56 (1964), pp. 109, 114; cf. also *Institutio Generalis Missalis Romani,* promulgated by a Decree of the Sacred Congregation of Rites on 6 April 1969, 33, and what has been said above in Chapter VI concerning the homily.

[118] Since the High Middle Ages, provincial councils have insisted on the responsibility of parents in regard to education in the faith: cf. Sixth Council of Arles (813), Canon 19; Council of Mainz (813), Canons 45, 47; Sixth Council of Paris (829), Book 1, Chapter 7: MANSI, *Sacrorum Conciliorum Nova et Amplissima Collectio,* XIV, 62, 74, 542. Among the more recent documents of the Magisterium, note the Encyclical *Divini Illius Magistri* of Pius XI, 31 December 1929: *AAS* 22 (1930), pp. 49-86; the many discourses and messages of

which should begin from the children's tenderest age,[119] is already being given when the members of a family help each other to grow in faith through the witness of their Christian lives, a witness that is often without words but which perseveres throughout a day-to-day life lived in accordance with the Gospel. This catechesis is more incisive when, in the course of family events (such as the reception of the sacraments, the celebration of great liturgical feasts, the birth of a child, a bereavement) care is taken to explain in the home the Christian or religious content of these events. But that is not enough: Christian parents must strive to follow and repeat, within the setting of family life, the more methodical teaching received elsewhere. The fact that these truths about the main questions of faith and Christian living are thus repeated within a family setting impregnated with love and respect will often make it possible to influence the children in a decisive way for life. The parents themselves profit from the effort that this demands of them, for in a catechetical dialogue of this sort each individual both receives and gives.

Pius XII; and above all the texts of the Second Vatican Council: the Dogmatic Constitution on the Church *Lumen Gentium*, 11, 35: *AAS* 57 (1965), pp. 15, 40; the Decree on the Apostolate of the Laity *Apostolicam Actuositatem*, 11, 30: *AAS* 58 (1966), pp. 847, 860; the Pastoral Constitution on the Church in the Modern World *Gaudium et Spes*, n. 52: *AAS* 58 (1966), p. 1073; and especially the Declaration on Christian Education *Gravissimum Educationis*, 3: *AAS* 58 (1966), p. 731.
    [119] Cf. Second Vatican Council, Declaration on Christian Education *Gravissimum Educationis*, 3: *AAS* 58 (1966), p. 731.

Family catechesis therefore precedes, accompanies and enriches all other forms of catechesis. Furthermore, in places where anti-religious legislation endeavours even to prevent education in the faith, and in places where widespread unbelief or invasive secularism makes real religious growth practically impossible, "the Church of the home"[120] remains the one place where children and young people can receive an authentic catechesis. Thus there cannot be too great an effort on the part of Christian parents to prepare for this ministry of being their own children's catechists and to carry it out with tireless zeal. Encouragement must also be given to the individuals or institutions that, through person-to-person contacts, through meetings, and through all kinds of pedagogical means, help parents to perform their task: the service they are doing to catechesis is beyond price.

At school

69. Together with and in connection with the family, the school provides catechesis with possibilities that are not to be neglected. In the unfortunately decreasing number of countries in which it is possible to give education in the faith within the school framework, the Church has the duty to do so as well as possible. This of course concerns first and foremost the Catholic

---

[120] Second Vatican Council, Dogmatic Constitution on the Church *Lumen Gentium*, 11: *AAS* 57 (1965), p. 16; cf. Decree on the Apostolate of the Laity *Apostolicam Actuositatem*, 11: *AAS* 58 (1966), p. 848.

school: it would no longer deserve this title if, no matter how much it shone for its high level of teaching in non-religious matters, there were justification for reproaching it for negligence or deviation in strictly religious education. Let it not be said that such education will always be given implicitly and indirectly. The special character of the Catholic school, the underlying reason for it, the reason why Catholic parents should prefer it, is precisely the quality of the religious instruction integrated into the education of the pupils. While Catholic establishments should respect freedom of conscience, that is to say avoid burdening consciences from without by exerting physical or moral pressure, especially in the case of the religious activity of adolescents, they still have a grave duty to offer a religious training suited to the often widely varying religious situations of the pupils. They also have a duty to make them understand that, although God's call to serve him in spirit and truth, in accordance with the commandments of God and the precepts of the Church, does not apply constraint, it is nevertheless binding in conscience.

But I am also thinking of non-confessional and public schools. I express the fervent wish that, in response to a very clear right of the human person and of the family, and out of respect for everyone's religious freedom, all Catholic pupils may be enabled to advance in their spiritual formation with the aid of a religious instruction dependent on the Church, but which, according to the circumstances of different countries, can be offered either by the school or in the setting of the school, or again within the framework of an agreement with the public authorities regarding school timetables, if catechesis takes place only in the parish or in another pastoral centre. In fact, even in places where objective difficulties exist, it should be possible to arrange school timetables in such a way as to enable the Catholics to deepen their faith and religious experience, with qualified teachers, whether priests or lay people.

Admittedly, apart from the school, many other elements of life help in influencing the mentality of the young, for instance, recreation, social background and work surroundings. But those who study are bound to bear the stamp of their studies, to be introduced to cultural or moral values within the atmosphere of the establishment in which they are taught, and to be faced with many ideas met with in school. It is important for catechesis to take full account of this effect of the school on the pupils, if it is to keep in touch with the other elements of the pupils' knowledge and education; thus the Gospel will impregnate the mentality of the pupils in the field of their learning, and the harmonization of their culture will be achieved in the light of faith. Accordingly I give encouragement to the priests, religious and lay people who are devoting themselves to sustaining these pupils' faith. This is moreover an occasion for me to reaffirm my firm conviction that to show respect for the Catholic faith of the young to the extent of facilitating its education, its implantation, its consolidation, its free profession and practice would certainly be to the honour of any Government, whatever be the system on which it is based or the ideology from which it draws its inspiration.

Within organizations

70.   Lastly, encouragement must be given to the lay associations, movements and groups, whether their aim is the practice of piety, the direct apostolate, charity and relief work, or a Christian presence in temporal matters. They will all accomplish their objectives better, and serve the Church better, if they give an important place in their internal organization and their method of action to the serious religious training of their members. In this way every association of the faithful in the Church has by definition the duty to educate in the faith.

This makes more evident the role given to the laity in catechesis today, always under the pastoral direction of their Bishops, as the Propositions left by the Synod stressed several times.

Training institutes

71.   We must be grateful to the Lord for this contribution by the laity, but it is also a challenge to our responsibility as Pastors, since these

lay catechists must be carefully prepared for what
is, if not a formally instituted ministry, at the
very least a function of great importance in the
Church. Their preparation calls on us to organize
special Centres and Institutes, which are to be
given assiduous attention by the Bishops. This
is a field in which diocesan, interdiocesan or
national cooperation proves fertile and fruitful.
Here also the material aid provided by the richer
Churches to their poorer sisters can show the
greatest effectiveness, for what better assistance
can one Church give to another than to help it
to grow as a Church with its own strength?

I would like to recall to all those who are
working generously in the service of the Gospel,
and to whom I have expressed here my lively
encouragement, the instruction given by my
venerated predecessor Paul VI: "As evangelizers,
we must offer ... the image of people who are
mature in faith and capable of finding a meeting-
point beyond the real tensions, thanks to a shared,
sincere and disinterested search for truth. Yes,
the destiny of evangelization is certainly bound
up with the witness of unity given by the Church.
This is a source of responsibility and also of
comfort".[121]

[121] Apostolic Exhortation *Evangelii Nuntiandi*, 77: *AAS* 68
(1976), p. 69.

CONCLUSION

72.   At the end of this Apostolic Exhortation, the gaze of my heart turns to him who is the principle inspiring all catechetical work and all who do this work—the Spirit of the Father and of the Son, the Holy Spirit.

In describing the mission that this Spirit would have in the Church, Christ used the significant words: "He will teach you all things, and bring to your remembrance all that I have said to you".[122] And he added: "When the Spirit of truth comes, he will guide you into all the truth ... he will declare to you the things that are to come ".[123]

The Spirit is thus promised to the Church and to each Christian as a Teacher within, who, in the secret of the conscience and the heart, makes one understand what one has heard but was not capable of grasping: "Even now the Holy Spirit teaches the faithful", said Saint Augustine in this regard, "in accordance with each one's

[122] *Jn* 14 : 26.
[123] *Jn* 16 : 13.

spiritual capacity. And he sets their hearts aflame with greater desire according as each one progresses in the charity that makes him love what he already knows and desire what he has yet to know".[124]

Furthermore, the Spirit's mission is also to transform the disciples into witnesses to Christ: "He will bear witness to me; and you also are witnesses".[125]

But this is not all. For Saint Paul, who on this matter synthesizes a theology that is latent throughout the New Testament, it is the whole of one's "being a Christian", the whole of the Christian life, the new life of the children of God, that constitutes a life in accordance with the Spirit.[126] Only the Spirit enables us to say to God: "Abba, Father".[127] Without the Spirit we cannot say: "Jesus is Lord".[128] From the Spirit come all the charisms that build up the Church, the community of Christians.[129] In keeping with this, Saint Paul gives each disciple of Christ the instruction: "Be filled with the Spirit".[130] Saint Augustine is very explicit: "Both (our believing and our doing good) are ours because of the choice of our will, and yet both are gifts from the Spirit of faith and charity".[131]

---

[124] *In Ioannis Evangelium Tractatus*, 97, 1: PL 35, 1877.
[125] *Jn* 15 : 26-27.
[126] Cf. *Rom* 8 : 14-17; *Gal* 4 : 6.
[127] *Rom* 8 : 15.
[128] *1 Cor* 12 : 3.
[129] Cf. *1 Cor* 12 : 4-11.
[130] *Eph* 5 : 18.
[131] *Retractationum Liber I*, 23, 2: PL 32, 621.

Catechesis, which is growth in faith and the maturing of Christian life towards its fullness, is consequently a work of the Holy Spirit, a work that he alone can initiate and sustain in the Church.

This realization, based on the text quoted above and on many other passages of the New Testament, convinces us of two things.

To begin with, it is clear that, when carrying out her mission of giving cathechesis, the Church —and also every individual Christian devoting himself to that mission within the Church and in her name—must be very much aware of acting as a living pliant instrument of the Holy Spirit. To invoke this Spirit constantly, to be in communion with him, to endeavour to know his authentic inspirations must be the attitude of the teaching Church and of every catechist.

Secondly, the deep desire to understand better the Spirit's action and to entrust oneself to him more fully—at a time when "in the Church we are living an exceptionally favourable season of the Spirit", as my Predecessor Paul VI remarked in his Apostolic Exhortation *Evangelii Nuntiandi* [132]—must bring about a catechetical awakening. For "renewal in the Spirit" will be authentic and will have real fruitfulness in the Church, not so much according as it gives rise to extraordinary charisms, but according as it leads the greatest possible number of the faithful, as they

[132] 75: *AAS* 68 (1976), p. 66.

travel their daily paths, to make a humble, patient and persevering effort to know the mystery of Christ better and better, and to bear witness to it.

I invoke on the catechizing Church this Spirit of the Father and the Son, and I beg him to renew catechetical dynamism in the Church.

Mary, Mother and Model
of the Disciple

73.   May the Virgin of Pentecost obtain this for us through her intercession. By a unique vocation, she saw her Son Jesus "increase in wisdom and in stature, and in favour".[133] As he sat on her lap and later as he listened to her throughout the hidden life at Nazareth, this Son, who was "the only Son from the Father", "full of grace and truth", was formed by her in human knowledge of the Scriptures and of the history of God's plan for his people, and in adoration of the Father.[134] She in turn was the first of his disciples. She was the first in time, because even when she found her adolescent son in the Temple she received from him lessons that she kept in her heart.[135] She was the first disciple above all else because no one has been "taught by God" [136] to such depth. She was "both mother and disci-

---

[133] Cf. *Lk* 2 : 52.
[134] Cf. *Jn* 1 : 14; *Heb* 10 : 5; S. Th. III, Q. 12, a. 2; a. 3, ad 3.
[135] Cf. *Lk* 2 : 51.
[136] Cf. *Jn* 6 : 45.

ple", as Saint Augustine said of her, venturing to add that her discipleship was more important for her than her motherhood.[137] There are good grounds for the statement made in the Synod Hall that Mary is "a living catechism" and "the mother and model of catechists".

May the presence of the Holy Spirit, through the prayers of Mary, grant the Church unprecedented enthusiasm in the catechetical work that is essential for her. Thus will she effectively carry out, at this moment of grace, her inalienable and universal mission, the mission given her by her Teacher: "Go therefore and make disciples of all nations".[138]

With my Apostolic Blessing.

Given in Rome, at Saint Peter's, on 16 October 1979, the second year of my pontificate.

Joannes Paulus PP. II

---

[137] Cf. *Sermo* 25, 7: *PL* 46, 937-938.
[138] *Mt* 28 : 19.

100